Time to Change

A guide to life after greed

Annie Davison

Time to Change

A guide to life after greed

Annie Davison

BOOKS

Winchester, UK
Washington, USA

First published by O-Books, 2011
O-Books is an imprint of John Hunt Publishing Ltd., Laurel House, Station Approach,
Alresford, Hants, SO24 9JH, UK
office1@o-books.net
www.o-books.com

For distributor details and how to order please visit the 'Ordering' section on our website.

ISBN: 978 1 84694 939 5

A CIP catalogue record for this book is available from the British Library.

Design: Lee Nash

Printed in the UK by CPI Antony Rowe
Printed in the USA by Offset Paperback Mfrs, Inc

We operate a distinctive and ethical publishing philosophy in all
areas of our business, from our global network of authors to
production and worldwide distribution.

CONTENTS

'The truth lies in seeing ourselves as Art not Power'

Muriel Barber: *The Elegance of the Hedgehog*

"I open my eyes to see that the sea is thick with darkness more than ever now, and the sky is grown somewhere beyond the paleness of the muted blue, stretching to be like the nothingness before all opposition first began – before there was either past or future to consume us in either memory or anticipation, when we could have lived in some loved suspension of the swollen moment, a thing more than enough, without the need for either a falling back, or a reaching forwards, just a steadiness there forever."

Candida Clark: *The Mariner's Star*

INTRODUCTION

It has been the nature of humanity since the beginning of time, to live within a principle of sparring duality, however you describe it – night and day, dark and light. The greatest duality, of course, is that we live as men and women, the relationship on which we project so many lessons for growth.

But I believe the over-riding task for humanity on earth is the integration of spirit and matter; in order to unravel a little more of the great mystery of what it is to be human. To do so we must first explore the unconscious – the depository of all our personal, tribal, family, and collective history – that lures us into destructive and limiting modes of behaviour and habitual reactive responses.

The unacknowledged depths of the unconscious cause us to live our lives as automatons, governed by fear and retribution, even when we think we are free or kicking against such restrictions. As the darkness lightens and we see ourselves consciously in a new light of spiritual awareness, it is possible to know real freedom, creativity and choice.

* * *

My eyes began opening to the psychic and spiritual gaze in the early 1970s. For me there was, on reflection, a natural progression from a yearning to understand my own chaotic emotionality, to a growing sense of empathy with others, to a deepening perception of how things are. That led to this opening to spirituality, triggered by an astrological reading with Frederic Davies.

As he revealed things about me nobody else could know, I saw that 'something out there' knew more about me than I did, and that the universe comprised a much bigger reality than I had ever imagined. It was as though a trap door was released above my head and I could move out from the frustrations and limitations of ordinary life. At the same time I 'knew with certainty' that this opening concerned two things. The first was that this was signalling the emergence and the profound depth and meaning of the 'feminine principle'. The second was that this opening to 'knowing' concerned the inevitable collapse of ideas, structures, and institutions founded on greed.

My journey to 'the feminine' – and opening to what I then called 'the higher self' and the Jungian concept of the supercon-scious – began immediately, and led to the publishing of my first book *The Wise Virgin* in 1979 (written as Annie Wilson).

The journey had been bizarre (certainly more bizarre than I could have wished for myself), often painful – because changes in consciousness do not come without risk and courage – but it was also exciting and full of adventure. As part of the 'me' generation and with the requisite self-absorption, I had followed the story of my own life very closely! I was the observer of my life, as well as the participant, reading my truths in my own process.

In 1995 I began to work as a channel. Channelling is an uncomfortable word because it has many connotations and misinterpretations. In fact, I saw channelling as just the latest outcome of a long journey of consciousness; opening up more and more to the complexities of 'accessing information' from other dimensions with increasing confidence, clarity and truth. I could not do it without the conviction that I have cleared my psyche to the best of my ability.

Channelling is like being the modem, connected to a vast broadband network, and providing a ripple-down effect from the finest to the densest atmosphere here on earth, passing on information that people can accept and understand. For the purposes of this book the guides refer to themselves as The Lords of Time. I have no objection to that, but I leave it to the reader to experience the level of consciousness for him or herself and come to his or her own conclusion.

For me the levels and applications of my guidance have changed and been 'upgraded' several notches over the years. I have learned to trust the wisdom of the information I am given in the moment and have offered to others, predominantly through individual client work and workshops.

One of my main motivations, right from the beginning, was to show the distinction between the psychic and spiritual realms. I had seen too much of the pulling power of psychic people, often unconsciously played out through the sexual chakra. I had witnessed the knots with which teachers of wisdom and healing had tied up their students or disciples.

I had also known, as a child, the darkness and fear of unwittingly tapping into the psychic (I had had a bad accident at the age of seven and severely knocked my nervous system). For years I was haunted by my own fears, which I learned later I had created into 'entities', and touched into the darker aspects of past lives.

So I felt it was my job to explain – at a time when the astral realms were beginning to open up for many more people – that, to my mind, there was often danger in the psychic. It was a myriad experience (as indeed is this thing called channelling) often involving the trickster. Human beings are so much more

3

than we can ever imagine.

We can link into disembodied aspects of ourselves that seem to give messages that we then assume are spiritual contact, but this is psychic and not necessarily pure. Without the commitment to the psychological and spiritual cleansing and clearing of the unconscious, we are capable of clouding, glamorising and playing with truth.

The spiritual is necessarily psychic but the psychic is not necessarily spiritual. The spiritual is the superconscious experience, of 'knowing' the Divine nature of humanity. It demands nothing less than everything in the pursuit of integrity, clarity and sheer hard work, in order to clear the persuasive unconscious of its manipulative habits. We try so hard to avoid change, to keep the status quo, and stay on our self-negating or over-inflating emotional tightropes.

* * *

The present moment marks a time of huge change, an opportunity for mankind to metamorphose into a new kind of humanity at the dawn of a New Creation. It is a time of extreme agitation in the world as a whole.

Many years ago it was indicated by serious people in the field of mind, body and spirit, that humanity had only a certain amount of time to work on the astral plane, that is, the damaging emotional levels of the unconscious. It was imperative to risk letting go our primitive urges and fears in order to find and establish a level of integrity, inspired by knowledge of a spiritual or 'Divine' *raison d'être*.

With the huge uprising of psychotherapy and 'growth movement' work in the seventies and eighties, it had become apparent to a groundswell of people that there was an urgency to 'clear the decks'.

Now, as if in justification of the sacrifices this journey

demanded, it would appear, in the current heightened crescendo of chaos, that changes are happening – and will happen – which give even more people very little choice. Clearly a change of heart is now urgently needed.

When my 'certainty' and opening to consciousness came in the seventies, I lived 'the feminine' journey for the next twenty years. It was many years later that the significance of 'the Goddess' became more or less mainstream. My second 'certainty': the question – and challenge – of greed, has taken over thirty years to seem 'current'.

What I intend here is a short history of Now. It is a simple discussion of the way things are at the present time, and is offered in the role of mentor. To be a mentor does not mean having every fact and figure at your fingertips. A mentor endeavours to have wise words for those who need moving and shaking, rather than chapter and verse of everything that is happening in their lives. Mentoring is a smaller task and a smaller offering in many ways, while at the same time, paradoxically, offering something more powerful and more rewarding. Simplicity will have its effect.

This book to all intents and purposes is channelled and yet, in the sense that I understand channelling, it is entirely my own work. The two here are seamless.

Please note that where, for the sake of smoothness I have used 'he' or 'him', it goes without saying that I also mean 'she' and 'her'. I trust, also, that you easily distinguish between the 'we' of the Lords of Time, and the 'we' that indicates 'us', the rest of humanity! It is the form of the text to use both.

* * *

In terms of how to read this book and understand the evolution of consciousness to this point, it requires simply that you open up to the imagination and suspend disbelief in the words that are being spoken here. The imagination is a tool of more power and holds more treasure than anyone scientifically can trust in or measure or even take part in.

In order to 'take apart' as the scientists are wont to do, they cannot open out, expand and enter into what is already there. In the idea and experimentation of the small and the even smaller – as in nano-technology, for example – scientists are actually exploring in the opposite direction to that which the imagination dares to roam. The world of the imagination is expansive of the whole, not divisive of the whole.

Consciousness is the dimension in which imagination has its widest aperture, and the wider the aperture, the higher, the broader, the bigger the experience can be of what it is to be conscious. Imagination has such a broad range; it has so many bandwidths of understanding. And as the imagination expands and expands, it is possible to recognise more and more of what it is to be human and the pivotal point of the universe.

Those scientists that have expanded scientific consciousness the most, are those who have unwittingly or wittingly expanded their imagination and not merely 'whittled down' through scientific analysis. If you imagine yourself whittling down and whittling down to the last halfpenny, like Scrooge, it feels small and mean, nitpicking and bitter, doesn't it? But by expanding the imagination you allow in and bring to view a world that is full of loving kindness, not the greed, distortion and disdain that many people experience at this time.

The purpose of this book, of this era, and the most significant task for humanity at this time, is to establish throughout the universe the resonance of loving kindness. There is an imperative for the loving kindness that is God, to be earthed from source. Through a magnetic pull from the source, via all planetary systems, ours is the only planetary system that can magnetise that earthing.

As the information resounds through all the systems, nearing its goal it begins resounding back. As this broad spectrum of energy reflects back to source, much of the darkest energy is 'fine-tuned' out, as if it becomes irrelevant. So in effect, receiving and reflecting back brings constant change. As the earth changes so does the universe. It is a two-way flow into the meaning of universal loving kindness.

PART ONE:

A SHORT HISTORY OF NOW

"We are the Lords of Time. We are the generation after the original Masters of Wisdom. We came into being at the Big Bang and the beginning of space-time."

What chance is there of alien life in the universe? What chance that there is a planet sufficiently like earth to support intelligent life? The scientists are reaching a crescendo of expectation. Some say it is more and more likely with the increasingly powerful instruments we have searching out in space. Others have almost given up, and say if they haven't contacted us by now, then they probably don't exist.

What scientists cannot do, it seems, is think laterally! Or outside the box!

Within the universe there are many conscious beings now trying to contact humanity, intelligences that are waiting to be contacted, in order to bring the world of humanity to its senses. There are those who already have an innate sense of the nature of our multidimensional world and are trying hard to bring their consciousness to a state of readiness. It behoves those who are caught up in the vagaries of modern consumerism to listen carefully now to the whispers of their own conscience.

SIMPLICITY

It is time for change. It is time to exchange our constant discourse around consumerism for a discourse on the art of living. The art of living is the art of simplicity in form and content. Simplicity is the key to more and more complex relationships on planet earth.

Why simplicity? Each individual has a keynote. And it is that keynote that sounds the nature of humanity as a varied and beautiful structure that makes a whole symphony of communication for universal intelligence. It is a simple matter for each human being to find their key note – made much more difficult when each individual has the idea that they are significant in their own right and not as a member of the human race.

Consumerism brings distinction of personality. In this day and age, the more an individual consumes the more superior they feel. The less an individual consumes, the more he or she considers him or herself inferior. What nonsense. Why does this happen?

When an individual incarnates on the planet they are in a state of grace. Very shortly after that the individual's burdens of identity from many, many lifetimes begin to impinge on God's grace and open up the individual to a life of raw and bloody response to the extent of that woundedness.

No one escapes the journey of retribution and redemption. No one. However, when the battle becomes too dangerous, or the individual is unable to stand the heat, consumerism is a marvellous displacement therapy. Consumerism has come at a time when there is an urgency to face those demons, to face the change of humanity. Why then do those without money also feel unable to face their demons? Because the need in them is so great that they live a life of envy and greed and self-aggrandisement.

Be careful what you wish for. Many, many people are living lives that in a moment of weakness they have called upon themselves. No one is exempt from self-responsibility, even if the wishes they make in an unconscious state are unconsciously drawn.

Consciousness, then, is the key to understanding. Consciousness is the tool that mankind possesses to move into the realms of the magical and multidimensional beauty that the world is now entering.

MATTER

Let us begin at the beginning.

Recently the most obvious accent has been on the globalisation of matter. Matter is the material world in which the human being takes for granted that he is the master of manifestation. However, when the material is manipulated to the extent that globalisation manipulates matter, the world takes on a patina of corruption.

Dealing only in matter always corrupts energies in the

environment. When matter is manipulated there is a corruption of energy that invades the whole environment. Corruption is the linchpin of matter. However, at this time a complete revolution is happening in the world today. Man has come to the zenith of his power to corrupt matter, so much so that his conscience is beginning to usurp his need for material gain.

There is revolution in the air, a complete change of dynamics, in which the human being has come to his senses and will from now on take matter very seriously indeed: matter as the relationship between God and humanity, and therefore in great need of spiritualisation. In other words, the God-self in matter must now be realised.

A tall order you may think. But in the coming years there will be a complete revelation that man can no longer corrupt matter to the extent that he has in the past. Global warming, collapse of institutions, are the warning signs that man cannot live by bread alone. Too much bread, more bread than the next man; every bread that is available is available to me. No matter how much bread you give me it is not enough. That leads to corruption.

For more centuries than anyone can account for, there has been the increasing tendency towards the total corruption of earth, through the opportunism that facilitates the corruption of matter. It has been the instinct of humanity, since man crawled out of the sea, to capitalise on matter; to find the main chance; to reach for the stars through corruption of matter.

But... humanity has come of age. Matter is at its most corrupt and people can no longer support the theory that what is mine is mine and I want more of it. It is time to recognise that man's job now is to spiritualise matter, to bring God down to earth, and for man to live in harmony with matter, if he is to live in harmony with the rest of mankind and in harmony with God.

We are all in this together now. Globalisation has made sure of that. Out of the negative comes the greatest positive, if only man could see what globalisation really means. The bringing together of mankind in the service of the good, the spiritualisation of matter and the harmony of mankind through God's loving kindness.

Impossible you may think. But in every man, woman and child on this earth there is a point of no return here. No one will benefit any longer by perpetuating the crime of corruption. Matter feeds on itself and man will begin to feed on himself, within himself in a way that no longer brings happiness or the taste for acquisitiveness by manipulating matter. The corrupt landlords of the planet will no longer prosper.

What does that mean? It means that those people, who are already living a disciplined and lonely life of service and understanding, will take their place as the leaders and encouragers of the others who are beginning to flap their wings in time with the truly changing times.

There is a clock ticking towards the time of change, when mankind realises himself to be a member of a multidimensional and loving universe that has an agenda of change and distinction to come. Mankind is the key to an evolving universe that is determined to run a tight ship now, in order to emerge into the twenty-first century as a universe of loving kindness, fed by the changing nature of man on earth.

We are the Lords of Time and it is now that we are making our appearance in Time, in order to facilitate this change of mind and heart in mankind. Who are we? We wish to tell mankind that Time is a construct and we are that construct. We are happy now that the moment has come to introduce the concept that time can no longer visit earth in the same way that it has over the last millennia, since the beginning of time.

Time is life everlasting and more and more people will begin to recognise that they are living in more dimensions than simply what they experience in their newly emerging twenty-first century. They can also roam in the realms of the gods or the ancestors at will. Yes, time travel is now becoming a fact of human life, so that man may begin to understand universal laws that are opening up to the gaze of humankind in the twenty-first century.

New time needs new understanding, that mankind has the ability to exist simultaneously in all planes, in all dimensions and in all regions of the universe.

WHY NOW?

Let's hold on a moment; make time for an explanation of why this information is significant at a time of extraordinary upheaval and change. Because it affects everyone's lives now, whether they know it or not, and because a real chasm is opening up between the greedy variety of humanity and those with integrity of matter and soul. There needs to be an understanding that the individuals with integrity will lead the way now.

Why now? For 2000 years religion has held the hearts and minds of humanity in the rigid grip of laws that govern man's endeavours to be 'good'. In endeavouring to be good, religions have fought for supremacy with religious wars, the cause of more bloodshed than territorial wars. Religion has reached its zenith. The idea of good is changing. The nature of God itself is changing.

Making the most of what you have is the most important request we make of humanity at this time. It is the edict by which all people of great virtue need to comprehend life. The trouble is, no one realises exactly how much they do have. In every human being are capacities beyond anything they can imagine in their current lives.

The way humanity sees itself right now is so limited that in the years to come people will wonder how they could possibly have chased the dreams they dream now. In the future mankind will reflect on this particular period as a whirl of chaotic dreams, mushing into a heap of nonsense.

People will reflect on this period as if in a haze of madness.

What we predict is that very soon those of integrity and understanding will be leading our world into a renaissance of understanding and captivating enjoyment, knowing that human beings are miracles of creation, and it is time to recognise them as such.

Soon the psychic gaze will blossom into a spiritual understanding that mankind has powers of perception, intuition and remarkable virtues that will lead all who are willing to recognise themselves to be Gods on Earth. Yes, Gods on Earth. Within every human being are universal forces that create a magnificence of harmony that can introduce God's vision to earth's understanding.

In ten years time the focus on virtue rather than greed will dominate the cultural drawing-rooms of all main political parties. There will be a massive clearout of non-virtuous people into the wilderness of thought. And everyone who enters the frame as a leader of men will have had a grounding in the spiritual nature of man.

When political virtue rests in the hands of those who have a basis in spiritual matters, no one will feel discarded or excluded from the nature of political decision-making. The rights of man will depend more on the inner relationship of those with virtue to their unseen mentors, than the vagaries of human emotional dependency.

Where are these men and woman? In the ethers. What we mean by this is that for many, many people their spiritualised selves are simply waiting to ensoul them on earth. Millions of spiritualised souls are being made ready in the multidimensional realms, ready to enter earth's atmosphere and move the energy of humanity into the glorious future of mankind. Does that sound scary? Not at all.

There are those in incarnation who have already incarnated several times in this one life. They have made way for their superior selves to enter their bodies and to begin the work of humanizing, or spiritualising mankind. These are not aliens, although aliens might be what they seem to be. They are the spiritualised bodies of men and women of virtue who over their current lifetimes have worked and worked to offer themselves up, accepted the invitation to be their most beautiful and most enriched selves.

However, at this moment, no one, and we say no one, has reached the pinnacle of their achievements, or has yet given the highest of the gifts they are able to give in this lifetime, in this era of time. This is because the world has not been ready, has not yet been fully cleared of the grave darkness that has enveloped the world of men and women.

That time of darkness, of the outer manifestation of man's shadow, is coming to an end now. With the sweeping away of dark institutions, with the grave errors of judgement exposed and the will of men and women turned towards the integrity of mankind, those brave souls who have waited to bring in their highest of gifts will now open themselves up to public gaze and be seen to be leaders of mankind.

The meek shall inherit the earth. But by that inheritance we mean a gentle, pleasurable leadership that offers hope and gratitude, and demands a participation that until now has been impossible to achieve. You will see.

GLOBAL WARMING
A Lot Of Hot Air

In many ways the most important aspect of the now moment is the incidence of global warming. Global warming is the single most important factor in most people's minds right now because global warming is the most important *inner* factor in most people's lives.

By global warming we mean the level of rage that is mounting inside and outside the environment of mankind. Global warming is the outer manifestation of man's inner rage. Rage against the status quo; rage of the individual at his inability to reach the top of his expected goals; rage that mankind has come to a standstill on the possibility of finding ultimate satisfaction in this life; rage at the manifest disappointment within every human being. It is as though humanity as a whole feels it has been 'let down by God'. The frustration of 'not enough' is rife within mankind right now, and it leads to an inner rage, the like of which mankind has not seen since time immemorial. The frustration of not enough fills the airways, whether it is not enough food in Africa, or not enough satisfaction in love, in sex, in money, in reputation, in celebrity. Not enough manifests as inner rage in mankind today.

Not enough, however, is not what anybody thinks it is. Not enough is the frustration of a people, which has come so far from its spiritualised nature that it is yearning, yes, yearning to bring a measure of spiritualised comfort into its innermost being.

'Not enough' is a cry for help. Rage is a fear response (think how hot you become when you become over-anxious). This outpouring of inner rage is in the ethers now. Witness the binge drinking, alcohol abuse, sexual abuse, and gang warfare. Unmitigated anger leads to abuse of all kinds, inner and outer, and the rage in the air is heating up the universe, as well as the earth itself.

However much scientists assuage the effects of global warming; however much the government offsets carbon footprints, there will be global warming. Nothing will change until mankind realises that its rage and heat is an inner rage, caused by a yearning to be let off the hook of frustration. It is people's yearning to have a deeper meaning to their lives, to become spiritualised beings, and in this way, ultimately, to find that they themselves are enough.

Electro-Magnetic Field
An important thing to understand at this time is that the world is going through the most incredible change of atmospheric

pressure. What the world experiences as global warming are the distortions and difficulties effected by a real 'upping' of the electro-magnetic field effect. As the electro-magnetic field ups the pressure in space, as it were, there is reduced pressure on earth.

Global warming is not about carbon emissions but about atmospheric pressure; a realignment of exterior pressure to interior pressure, which is changing the nature of the balance between matter and spirit. It is the changing pressure in the magnetic field that is affecting the weather as well as the climate, and adds to the tensions and anxieties people already feel.

If in an anxious state you touch your toes (actually or in your mind's eye), sense the changing pressure in your head. It is as though immediately the pressure goes away and you feel much calmer. There is a constant need in these changing times to earth the energy in this way. It is a need now to earth a *magnetic* charge instead of an electrical charge.

Imagine earthing an electrical charge through the root or groin area (like a lightning charge through a lightning conductor), you will feel a kind of electrical 'whiz' in the groin; a bang, a degree of excitement. But when you earth the magnetic charge by holding the feet, it is not like the tension of lightning conduction, it is the experience of calmness.

The magnetic field is now earthing in this much, much deeper way, experienced not just through the root chakra, but right through the earth, and destined to create a new possibility of peace on earth. What those of like mind and consciousness are doing now is earthing the magnetic field in a new way; like placing a 'net' around the earth and putting tent pegs in to hold it down securely. As you might put micromesh over your raised beds to protect your seeds from destructive pests, this net protects the earth from the negativities that creep in.

When the magnetic charge is earthed there is less pressure on earth. This new pressure heralds, most significantly, a new consciousness. The outcome of these changes is a more benign, purer and peaceful earth, safe from electrical discharges that hit the earth, and cause upset and explosions. Humans will no longer be predominantly electrical dischargers, but magnetic dischargers.

This will alter the way we relate to each other; we will be less karmically explosive, and much more gentle. It will be as though we mesh together to grow, rather than explode together to change.

THE NOW MOMENT

Each and every individual is enough in themselves, in their own sense of a spiritual, moral and creative identity. Simple you might think, but so difficult to achieve. Or is it?

Each time a person writes a birthday card there will be a sentiment of pleasure at writing to someone special. This feeling of pleasure is the feeling that permeates through humanity when there is a good sense of moral and spiritual welfare. Write a birthday card now, in your mind. Who would you send it to? Your mother, your father, your sister, your best friend? Then feel the warmth of writing some truly meaningful phrases for their particular well-being in life. Do you feel a warm glow of pleasure that you have been thinking positive and kind and warm thoughts for their birthday?

In fact that is all it takes to begin to understand that a warm feeling for everyone you meet is actually possible, with a little thought and understanding of their needs, their anxieties, their wish to be free to enjoy their lives in comfort, safety and under the glow of other peoples' good wishes.

Simple? Think about it. Do you ever really put that other person in front of you and examine what they truly need to make them happy and supported by what you have to say, or imply in your behaviour towards them?

Perhaps not. But in these days of chaos and uncertainty, it is this that will make all the difference in the world to other people's well-being. In fact it is the key to mankind's dilemmas at a time of huge transition, the transition towards understanding that the planet is becoming a place of real beauty and well-being, despite the signs to the contrary.

Children are being born who will take the planet to new heights of finesse and wisdom, despite the awful state of the world today. Oh yes, the children will do what the parents could only dream of in their wildest ideological fantasies.

Make the most of the life you've got. This is the truest advice we could ever give humanity today. Make the most of everything you have in detail, in simplicity. Look around you at every opportunity and see into the tiniest detail of your life and find the gem, the jewel of that existence for all it is worth. See yourself as the wisest person on earth, simply because you can find the jewel in the crown of your kingdom.

Realise today that what you have now is all you need. Tomorrow you may have more but that is tomorrow. It is today that matters. It is here, now, in the presence of who you are, that everything exists in the present moment. Reflect on the present moment; feel its impact on your whole being – now. Realise its presence as a motivational force for delight and pleasure and wisdom.

The present moment is the only one you have, for now, and it is perfectly poised to be the best moment in your life. Really and truly, this is the best moment in your life. Every present moment, this tiny particle of time, is the best in your life. Because the present moment will link you into the forever of human existence, past, present and future, where everything that is held in the fragility of humanity is safe, is true and honest.

Honesty is the best policy, because mankind's basic instinct for honesty is the one that will save everyone from the pitfalls of insecurity and discomfort in the end. Truth and beauty demand that each one of us is honest in everything we do: honesty in relationships and in dealing with our peers, in rooting in the soil of our life's work. Honesty with ourselves, with others and with every human being we come into contact with.

NEW WORLD VIEW

We must take the opportunity handed to us right now, to look at everything in our world view and change it. Um. Change everything in our world view? That seems a very hard task. And yet... we believe that everyone has the capability to change their world view in an instant. How could that be? An instant of time is the present now moment, and a change of heart, now, is all it takes to change the world.

The current view is that the world is a matter of separate systems, each competing with the other for supremacy. This is no longer fashionable or even possible. Today we must think of the world as a beautiful whole, a beautiful system in and of itself, rolling around in the universe as an integral part of everything that is. Astronauts who have seen earth from space report this kind of mystical understanding. We are part of that whole, part of that one system and wish now to remember ourselves as a part of one whole.

In the beginning, when the world became a unit in and of itself, and apparently separated from the whole in the Big Bang of this created universe, the earth felt separate and alone and different. But now its memory is returning. The earth is remembering that it began, in the deepest past, as part of one world, a universal world. It can remember itself as a whole, and that all its creatures – human and other – are simply part of everything that is, connected in every way, through DNA.

Yes, DNA. This is the strand of connection that is beginning to prove that we are part of each other, and of every living thing. We are closer to mice and men and to every living thing than we ever thought possible before the discovery of DNA.

So, it seems, I am my brother's keeper. If you don't like your brother, then change your heart. It doesn't mean you have to love your brother in a silly, non-essential way. It simply means that in your heart you are aware that he, like every other thing, is part of you; part of the great wide whole that you are privileged to exist in. Though you may actually dislike your brother, nonetheless you can love him as part of your life force, the part that connects you to the new and the whole. We are all in this together and as such must root for everyone else and wish that they, too, might become who they need to become, in the best and easiest way possible.

In the beginning God so loved the world that he made his only begotten 'son' – the human being – in his own image. As a result, we have tried for millennia to attain our God-selves. But in that trying we have come to realise that we are 'only human' after all. We have absolutely no chance at all of becoming like God. Or have we?

God made man not only in his own image, but also in the image of earth. Man's matter is the matter of earth itself, and it was through matter, on earth, that God wished to express Himself. But matter was gross and base. And it was the task of man to become the alchemist, to turn that base material into gold. It was an uphill task.

Millennia after millennia, lifetime after lifetime, man has returned to Earth School – the planet of love and healing – in order to understand the full meaning of the base material of his being, while striving and striving to become God.

And by these efforts of evolving consciousness over these millennia, the earth has become more and more spiritualised, in and of itself. The earth is 'warming up', in order to assume its heart-felt spiritualised self, made ready to receive the kind of humanity that God imagined for the most beautiful planet in the solar system.

You might think, on the contrary, that the earth is housing more and more monsters, with the appalling, chaotic things we see going on at this time. But in the paradoxical way of space-time existence, although mankind is playing out its worst side right now, underneath that layer, that miasma of chaos, a new world is forming. Soon, very soon, a new image of man will appear from behind that cloud, that miasma, and show us we are now in the most beautiful era that mankind has ever witnessed.

How can that be true? How can this miasma just disappear when it feels so entrenched, so miserably oppressive at this time? The answer is simple. It can happen when each man, woman and child with a modicum of misery in their souls, sees they are in the position to change their situation: simply by realising themselves as truly part of a magical, shifting world – including all creatures, great and small – and becoming aware of themselves as part of a magical whole.

When the world takes on the mantle of beauty, rather than love and healing, then will open up to each individual the most wonderful array of choices; choices that have not been available to mankind since time began.

LETTING GO

Many people at this time want to change their world view. And yet they are reluctant to give up even a modicum of what they already have and the image of what they think they are. There's the rub. Letting go is always difficult, and yet that is what needs to happen before anything new can come into focus. And how much more there is to give up for something as important as a new world view.

Our cherished identity has to be let go completely, with all the risk, fear and difficulty that entails, and no signposts to the future. How do we do that? How can we guarantee that in letting go the old, the new will unfold in the way we would wish it to? That is the thing: there is no guarantee.

So why should we bother?

We bother mainly when there is no option but to do so: when

there seems to be nothing to lose. It means we have come to the end of a particular phase in our life and everything begins to go wrong. When things start to go wrong, when the old simply cannot be sustained any longer, it is time to accept the inevitability of change. And in that second of decision, things do begin to change. Letting go becomes as inevitable as anything you have ever done, and you might as well go quietly. In other words, sit down; reflect on what needs to be let go, and then *let it go.*

For example – and most controversially – if you are married and the marriage is coming to an end, you may as well decide to end it, rather than go on for years and years, and even more years, hoping that it will change again. You will know whether it has the chance to change, or not, and being honest, facing the fear and doing it anyway, allows the soul to realign to its proper functioning again.

It is the nature of human beings to keep on changing, keep on growing. If that means the end of a marriage because all else has failed, then the soul is wanting that for you – and your partner and even for the children. Even if your excuse for not changing has been to hang on and on and on to something that is not working and ultimately is more destructive for all concerned.

Does that sound harsh? The world is a harsh learning sphere. And yet, what ultimately comes from all this learning is that the earth has been, and is, the place most suited for the lessons of love and healing. And now – as the new world view comes into force – earth is in the process of becoming a world of the most exquisite and loving beauty. That is the truth. The harsh world can be left behind, the greedy world can be left behind, and then into view comes a new world: the world of truth, beauty and loving kindness.

Why not look at the way the world is turning now? In a few years the work ethic will become a thing of the past. What the world needs is an ethic of retaining the means of production in every way possible, but the main ethic will be to see that every child is brought up in an environment of loving kindness, not as a means of production for the world to turn in the old way. The children born today are approaching a level of consciousness whereby they cannot be used simply to produce the world's goods, but will be seen as ambassadors for right thinking

There is a point to be made here. It is clear to see that any system that is failing begins to have a negative impact on the wider world. If there is a chance to become a better person, then now is the moment to make that a priority.

The air around us is ready for change – in every aspect of human conditioning, as we know it today. By the time the world wakes up to the fact that the world has changed, many people will have passed their sell-by date in terms of making that decision – to change their world view, and be open to a really happy and uncluttered life.

Those who have not made the decision to inhabit a bigger and better part of themselves, will feel they are under a cloud of unknowing. They will begin to feel they are 'out of the loop' and muddled, as far as their lives and preoccupations are concerned. It will feel odd indeed still to think of being 'number one', and to remain oblivious to the spiritual opening that is happening on earth as we speak.

CYCLES OF TIME

The book of memory is opening up to those who are ready to remember themselves as spiritual beings, and ready to become, in a way that they could never have imagined when they entered earth's atmosphere in this incarnation. It is a surprise even to those who were ready from birth to open themselves up to spiritual practices and spiritual unfolding.

What we have now is a new consciousness, a new recognition that man is already spiritualised, already able to touch the stars, already able to become the right hand of God. The children of today are opening up in readiness for an adventure of a lifetime; a journey towards the extension of consciousness throughout planet earth, and the experience of Life Everlasting, of Heaven on Earth.

Earth is the chosen planet. Earth has the exact configuration of atoms and molecules at this time to open up to a vast horizon of intergalactic understanding. The time has come, predicted by so many ancient traditions, for the world to expand its consciousness to understand what it is to be a signatory to inter-galactic communication.

It is time to warmly welcome all those who wish to take this opportunity, to become their fullest selves in this new and adventurous way. Our aim is to make sure that everyone who wishes to take this ride of a lifetime has everything they need for a warm, easy and comfortable journey.

So who are we? The Lords of Time are the workhorses of the universe. We take everything that has ever happened into our system of calculation and enjoy the task of ensuring that everything that has ever happened is recorded in the akashic records for all time.

When the time is right for a boost in consciousness for planet earth, we mete out the part of ancient history that needs to be taken into consideration before the next phase of consciousness can be understood and absorbed into earth's atmosphere. In other words, there are streams of experience that always need to be repeated and made conscious before the next phase of consciousness can take place in the collective that is Earth.

That is why there are cycles and cycles and cycles of experience. Like the cycles of the moon and the earth there are always cycles of experience that release the next phase of man's conscious ability to understand himself as a Master of Wisdom. For, indeed, the ultimate aim of consciousness is that all people of all time are able to take up the mantle of becoming Masters of Wisdom in their own right.

Once a planet called Earth has a full complement of Masters of Wisdom, these ambassadors are sent out to the stars of the infinite galaxies beyond galaxies beyond galaxies to spread that wisdom of love and beauty into the universal endlessness. No mean task, and one that humanity as a whole must and will become aware of, as the significance of this particular moment becomes more solidly based in man's understanding.

In the beginning, God so loved the world that he gave his only begotten son to earth consciousness. What became the Christmas story was in fact the repeat of another cycle of another cycle of another cycle. For God it was the endless story of man's task to become the ambassador of God's loving kindness through infinity.

He chose planet Earth for his own joy. Joy is the history of God made manifest on earth and the reason He chose the earth is because earth has the harmonic resonance for joy. No other planet has the same harmonic resonance necessary for joy. This is why Christianity, a religion that brought in joy, was so eagerly taken up by so many peoples. Christianity was the renewal of a cycle, and the opportunity for the Lords of Time to herald the coming of the consciousness of joy.

Joy, however, is only possible, through the understanding of suffering. What Christianity brought was the spiritual understanding of the crucifixion: of suffering and original woundedness. The history of humanity made manifest by the life of Jesus who became the Christ Everlasting.

What needed to happen at that time was the recognition of Earth as the planet of joy through the understanding of suffering. Thus the crucifixion was the last great happening, before the earth could understand itself as the planet of joy. God made manifest, through the birth of His son, the possibility of a fully spiritualised humanity on earth. The harmonics of earth would allow the joyous understanding: that man is the spiritualised experience of God on Earth.

MERCY NOT JUSTICE

How will we know joy? Through loving kindness. And we will know loving kindness through *mercy* not justice. Man's obsession with justice is a throwback to Old Testament ideals, and we dare to suggest that the main religions are full of Old Testament thinking.

It is true that justice was once far more 'humane' than mercy, but now, in fact, the opposite is true. Where once justice was the common purpose for good, it is now the principle of mercy that offers the most important prospect for global understanding. Mercy through loving kindness brings joy on earth.

How is that?

In the beginning was the word and the word was law. God was a God of justice. The 'fallen from grace' would not be ostracised but guided, and in the beginning guidance was given through law and justice. The 'Fallen Angel' led humanity away from God, on his journey to earth; through matter; through greed and consumption, to the limits of personal satisfaction and satiation.

And God meted out the law throughout, to bring the idea of justice foremost into the minds of the fallen ones – those brave souls who had elected to descend into matter and of necessity over eons of time to forget their spiritual God-self. In this way they could begin to prepare the earth for its manifest destiny, as the planet of joy and wisdom. Justice was the plan through which God could keep humanity on a tight rein, in order to complete its task of manifesting spirituality in earth, on earth and throughout earth's atmospheric presence.

Now the energies are changing and transmuting, and finer and finer energy is descending on to the planet. It is thanks to these experimenters, these adventurers, these brave souls whose task it has been, slowly but surely, to remember their God-self and ultimately to spiritualise matter.

The quality of mercy is no longer strained. Instead, mercy can become the global representative of God's loving presence and the way to each man's heart. Man is becoming aware that he now has the opportunity to take up the challenge of God's wish: for all men to be carriers of God's loving kindness in the new day of the new dawn of earth as the planet of truth, wisdom and beauty.

At the dawning of the new age of beauty, wisdom and truth, the word was *loving kindness*, which moves and has its being in mercy to all loving creatures. The 'love' we speak of in the old worldview, has become a bartering tool – a rule of law that says, 'if you love me, I will love you'. Over eons and eons of time this kind of love – conditional love – has become the bartering tool for love, money, sex, crime and independence of spirit.

So on the one hand, love has led to the independence of spirit, on the other, it has led to the idea that everything can be bought in this world of commodities. Now, however, the law of love is changing, from possessive, greedy love, to the love of detached loving kindness. Men and women of independent spiritual 'knowing' are realising that nothing can be bought, other than that which satisfies their immediate needs for survival.

Everything else needs only the understanding of loving kindness to bring it into being – according to the needs of that soul to do what it is undertaking to do in this particular lifetime.

Mercy, we suggest, is now making itself felt in earth's magnetic field, as a result of the work of those whose task has been to bring loving kindness into being. Mercy has such different energy to justice at this time. Until now man has carried such guilt that he needed to be punished by God. Plagued by this wish to punish himself and bring justice, he has projected injustice on others, and been merciless on himself. Going over and over what he did wrong, he finds no mercy.

But what happens when you feel mercy for yourself, not justice? With justice at your heels, it feels like sitting on a metal seat with spikes, which makes you rigid and stiff. With mercy to yourself the sword of justice just disappears and gives way to a very gentle approach, to understanding.

With mercy you feel much, much softer; the whole body relaxes; the blood pressure goes down. You feel well again. You feel like a good person. There is no dark hole, no darkness; there is no 'side'. When there is mercy rather than justice, you can see there is every possibility for goodness in the world. It is as though holding the mighty sword of justice has worn us out, but holding the hand of mercy allows humanity completely to revitalise in a new and wonderful way.

Mercy, then, begins at home: mercy and loving kindness towards oneself. Knowing yourself to be of great stature, of great beauty and without greed or hubris or wanting more than you need for a successful journey through this life of love, beauty, wisdom and truth.

Mercy, then, is the first reason to love yourself and believe in yourself as a beautiful creature of God's earth. Then, and only then, does the world become magical, illuminated, fairy-like to the touch. The walls begin to thin; the dimensions stretch into infinity and all creatures are in touch, through mercy, within and without, with incarnational truth.

Heaven opens in an instant through mercy. Heaven's gates are closed through justice. When God sits in judgement; when you sit in judgement – of yourself, of others, of the system – the walls close and imprison humanity in their own cells of self-dislike.

In the beginning man was fearful of his own nature. Indeed man was afraid of everything in his surroundings. Heaven was a thing to be feared; love was a thing to be feared; art was a thing to be feared, because everything was under the jurisdiction of an angry God; a God who judged the fallen ones, led by the Fallen Angel, the rebel angel Lucifer.

But God knew, too, that He had to accept the fall of the angelic realms, in order to bring about a heaven on earth. Through the auspices of the one who had the courage to leave God's loving kindness, the outpost of earth could be brought to

Life.

Many of the fallen angels were unable to lift their eyes to God because they were afraid. They were too afraid to know themselves in the mirror image of God himself. Fear led them to behave in a way that allowed them to believe they were at the mercy – or judgement – of God's wrath. Each individual would make himself an island unto himself and a target of God's wrathful world.

However, a merciful God was also waiting in the wings of time. As man has progressed on earth, the God of Judgement can become the God of Mercy. What was perceived as 'original sin' might now be understood at the deepest level as the perpetuation through time of the 'original wound'. God so loved his sons – the fallen angels of humanity – that he forgave their sins. But now, in the merciful eyes of heaven, man can be seen as the victim not the aggressor.

Those creatures, who began the descent, all those eons ago, were victims of God's ultimate plan – to bring heaven to earth. They faced their wounds of sacrificial love with fortitude. After eons of time, man is able now to let go his fear, repeated lifetime after lifetime through the five 'original wounds' of what it has meant to be human: felt within each of us as rejection, abandonment, abuse, denial or betrayal by God.

Man can now forgive God.

JUST IN TIME

Humanity was in a state of grace until man's 'fall from Grace' at the beginning of Time. Time has only been present on earth for a relatively short period in this dimensional reality.

Relatively speaking time is a new phenomenon, and only exists in the sphere of planet earth. That is why earth has become the repository of God's meaning for the universe. Time has stopped in some universes, and not begun in others. For this reason, earth is the focus of God's will to loving kindness and

His wish to become manifest in material dimensions as well as spiritual dimensions. Who would know God existed if there were no time?

Time is the essential that makes earth a perfect repository for goodness at its deepest resonance of meaning. The evolution of consciousness towards intrinsic goodness comes through man's own efforts throughout the course of time. Goodness can only be truly understood when time exists to manage the movement of time through all the dimensions that have the task of routing goodness through time.

Marvellous moments of discovery could not be registered without the movement of time. Moments of discovery are the engines of evolutionary thought. It is time that makes a distinction between these marvellous moments, and records the progress of humanity. It enables us to measure our ability to take on more and more of God's essence: to take on universal wisdom and understanding.

Time now is of the essence because timing is everything in the discovery of God's heart in matter. Time is of the essence because time is changing on planet earth. It is moving on to other dimensions that also need time to discover themselves as ambassadors of God's will and loving kindness. Time is short.

This does not mean the end of the world. Man will not disappear. The earth will not disappear. But as the speeding up of time gathers apace and the earth itself changes radically, through global warming; through the sun's activity and man's progress through time, time will no longer have the capacity for registering the progress of man towards loving kindness in the old way.

In other words, time in its original form has allowed the history of God to be registered in the human framework, in order for humanity to reach integration with God's intention and enter into the timeless dimension of universal loving kindness. The vastness and intelligence of universal loving kindness will now be the main focus of humanity's experience on earth. The small picture of day-to-day discovery, or movement through, or progress or growth, will no longer be the same powerful tool of earth's existence as it was before.

THE BIGGER PICTURE

The fact of the credit crunch and low-growth models will become the norm in human society. There will be less consumption, less rampaging greed and growth and fairer distribution. There will be more enjoyment of the simple, simply because life will be lived in a vastness of universal understanding and time itself will be less relevant to the majority of mankind.

Those still gripped by the marches of time will feel less empowered, not more empowered. While those who choose to live in the vastness of universal understanding, will be happy with less and less, have less and less and still feel empowered. They will enjoy the simplicity of knowing they are held in thrall by a bigger universal system, whereby they can take part in the glorious integration of spirit and matter and all that this entails for creative freedom and spiritual understanding.

This world is not the only world that has life. But life on other planets is different. Life on planet earth is so specific, so finely tuned that only life on earth can exist on earth. However, in other spheres of the universe, life is not so specific. Consciousness can and does exist is a less rarefied way: a less specific, less material way than on earth. In other words, consciousness does not depend on matter and the specifics of matter, to exist in other spheres.

Which is why the scientists looking for life 'out there' are not looking in the right places. They are looking from a material point of view, not a consciousness point of view. We exist in time immemorial, which means we are not in space-time, but in consciousness time. You will soon begin to see that you are looking in the wrong manner for life on Mars, for example. There is life on Mars; there is life on Venus and Jupiter and Saturn and out and out and out, beyond the solar system, into galaxy after galaxy after galaxy.

The universe is a living, breathing, active, dynamic force that measures itself in time immemorial not in metres and centimetres and metric tonnes and all the parameters peculiar to earth. Earth is so specific, so densely formed, so matter of fact, and seemingly so far away from the matter of belief and understanding and consciousness, and the inner regions of exploration.

We, the Lords of Time, are alive and well in time immemorial. Which is why we can help planet earth to understand its unique and specific purpose in the universe. But help it to understand, too, that it is not the only game in town. Life, in universal terms, exists in multidimensional realms of fantastical proportions. It is the world of the imagination – fantasy even – that is now reaching out to earth for communication and consciousness.

We are the cyberspace community – without a need for computers! We are wired and wired and wired throughout the universal system of communication, which can be reached so easily. And yet with such difficulty, because matter until now has prevented most human beings from soaring on the multidimensional waves of communication and listening to the music of the spheres through their imagination.

AGEING IS COOL

These days everyone on earth has the dream of staying young, or even becoming immortal. Ageing is such anathema to the majority of people on the planet at this time. There are so many creams and potions and so much demand for cosmetic surgery: the fight for anti-ageing is at its height of popularity. However, that was not always so in other realms. Age means wisdom, and wisdom is the source of all evolutionary conduits.

Ageing is not something to be dreaded in the way most

people do at this time. What happens in ageing is not just a loosening of physical faculties, but a refining of the spiritual powers. Let's look at it like that. Yes, there is a loosening of physical prowess, but if we understood the nature of consciousness, we would see that in trying to 'hold it all together' we are actually lessening our chances of taking an easy ride into old age. Above all, we are hampering the opportunity of engaging more and more with our ability to enter the best universe of all: that of universal understanding.

Think about it. As the physical body becomes less and less 'taut' and less able to hold the physical structure into alignment with the material world, so the faculty of consciousness and spiritual understanding is able more easily to merge into the physical structure of humanity. This is why ageing is such a prevalent subject at this time. The fear of losing physical tautness and structure is a fear of losing grasp on the physical world; the world of consumption and status, which are regarded as the epitome of life as it is lived today.

In ancient cultures, such as the Chinese, ageing was considered an honourable thing to do, a wise thing to do. There was great respect for the ageing population and their access to wisdom; not only the wisdom gained through a lifetime of experience, but also the wisdom that they were now open to, through the lessening of their physical tautness and structure.

The ageing population is actually the lucky population – if they grow old gracefully. Those who fight and struggle to maintain their youth – and naivety – may find themselves infantilising, through dementia and other devastating 'forgetting' difficulties connected with a fear of ageing.

However, those who are tranquil, calm and interested in the ageing process, will realise there is potential in their 'forgetting'. It allows them to 'remember' through other channels, the vastness of human life and the depths of their spiritual connectedness to the great beyond. It allows them to witness a far bigger and more exciting vision for life, than the smaller, diminishing picture they seem to live in now.

Allow ageing to be a happy time, a mortal time, while looking and having your being in the broader view of mankind, as a splendid, multidimensional creature. Experience the true beauty of man, whose head is in the clouds of unknowing, yet whose feet are grounded in vast acres of knowledge, wisdom and understanding. How beautiful is that? How beautiful is the ageing process, whereby man knows himself to be at one with the stars?

Paradoxically, there will be more ageing now than anyone ever thought, despite increasing longevity. People might be living longer, but many of the more debilitating diseases, normally attributed to older age, are visiting the body at a younger and younger age. Diabetes, back problems, multi-layered DNA difficulties are actually causing younger people to go through the ageing process earlier than might be expected in an era when longevity is expected to increase not diminish.

It means that more people are living with chronic illness earlier in their lives than they could possibly have imagined. Younger people are suffering with chronic back pain, colitis, Crones disease, and particularly, through obesity, are dealing with heart problems, waterworks problems, blood pressure problems, all diseases that until now have been strictly defined by older age.

In a way, ageing has become an emergency measure. Spiritual consciousness in this era is hard won, when there is so much idealisation of greed, celebrity and consumption. But the energy is changing so profoundly and so fast that mankind is now in a hurry to move with the changing times; to know itself as a higher mind, a spiritual being. The quickest way for some is through ageing; by letting go the rigidity of material structure they can 'reach the stars', inner as well as outer.

Once man returns to himself and lives as a higher being, these chronic diseases will recede in the young. The elderly will live fruitful, active lives into far greater age, as they are meant to do at this time. When we recognise this shift in energy and quietly let go the notion that greed and consumption are the way to our heart, the body itself will settle down. It can let go its tight hold on the material, and will change so radically that inner beauty and inner radiance will highlight true wonderment at our spiritual heritage and glorious future.

Ageing will ultimately be a thing of the past in terms of age being seen as unattractive and incompetent. Age will become loved and cherished and sought after. The opening into multidimensional experience will bring the recognition that we flow from one life to the next, one dimension to the next, alive or, what mortality calls, dead. We last, no matter what. We live no matter what.

LIGHTING UP

The ethers are crowded with dimensions that are living and breathing. We can exist in a glorious network of loving kindness. The incompetence, the insecurity, the fear, the darkness, the corruption and 'evil' are carried within man itself, not in the essence of universal loving kindness.

The layer of darkness around the earth, that essential wrath, is not of God but of man. For earth is the school of conscious spirituality and the awareness of spirit is the conscious understanding and integration of the duality of dark and light.

In fact, those holes in the ozone layer are the piercing by men of consciousness, into the realms of light. In this way the light of the spirit can enter earth's atmosphere and bring the light of consciousness to earth. What is seen and experienced by many people as a negative global impact is in reality a positive picture of earth's rising consciousness.

When more and more human beings bring in more and more light through the integration of spirit, so the earth will become increasingly powerfully attuned to light and the earth itself will 'take the heat' in a positive way.

Everything that is happening at this time is due to the earth's significance in the current unfolding of the universal plan. Yes, it is in the plan of universal unfolding that planet earth should become as rarefied in consciousness as the old empire of Sirius in the first universe. And at this time, Sirius B is the single most significant star for this solar system. It is currently the most energetic influence on planet earth.

In his book *The Sirius Mystery*, Robert Temple has written eloquently about the Dogon tribe in Africa who intuitively knew the vital influence Sirius B had on them, although it could not be seen. Earth now needs to recognise Sirius as the most positive over-lighting influence of the planet, in order for Light Everlasting to enter earth's atmosphere in the way it is meant to do at this time.

Light is the Mind; it is as simple as that. Light is the fuel that allows the mind of man to become conscious of itself as Light. Light is consciousness. Light is the understanding that man can raise his consciousness to the heights he was meant to do. The more the light of consciousness can enter the human body, the more conscious man can become aware that he is Divine. And that he has abilities to reach the stars, to be in the universe, the envoy of God Himself.

We all have the ability to be sons and daughters of God – in this life, on this planet, in this universe – and must be so in order for the universal mind of God to move up a gear; towards a new universe of pure light, tempered with the earthly gift of loving kindness.

Men and women of Light-mindedness can show others the way simply by lighting up the world. While man in general grubs along the bottom of his darkest nature, those of Light mind must still take the strain of earth's plan to raise man's nature up to the Light of God's plane. Light tempered with love is the ideal state of being: Light must be infused with earth's gift of loving kindness, so that earth does not burn itself out.

Who are these people of Light-mindedness? In fact there are many, many people in this world who have spent years and years and years of their current lives, and countless lives in eons past, to become conscious that they are now the carriers of pure Light Everlasting. And there are the millions who have caught the zeitgeist of God's loving kindness, who are not conscious of having done so.

Those who carry the light of God's loving kindness are legion, and yet it is only relatively few people who are conscious that they have done so. There are legions of people who have understood the law of magnetic-attraction, the law of 'as ye sow so shall ye reap', the law of 'like attracts like' and so on, in their daily lives, and have worked tirelessly for the good of mankind without thought for themselves at all.

But there are others who have worked tirelessly, too, in other ways: those who have worked on themselves, making themselves purer and purer and purer in terms of their own well-being and Light-heartedness. Through their innate recognition that man is Divine as well as material, they have pursued a path of consciousness, in order ultimately, through superhuman efforts and sacrifice, to become channels of pure light.

There are those who are conscious of their efforts, and pursue with integrity their journey to soul consciousness; and finally open up with consciousness to Light-heartedness. These are the people who, simply by being, are able to bring the rest of humanity into a state of consciousness, in a way that those who have merely acted in good faith and great-mindedness – without the raising of consciousness – are unable to do.

It is imperative now that the consciousness of mankind is raised, in order for him to reach and become the Light of the World. Happily, more and more people are expected to join this band of fellow travellers, because the situation on planet earth demands that they do so. It is no longer possible to eat the world's resources in such a huge and hungry bite of insecurity, and continue this obsession with values that are wrong for everyone at this time.

The tide is turning with many more people questing and searching for a way to idealise goodness and Light-heartedness. Yet still many are making that search without being prepared to give up anything of themselves in the process. However, amongst their number are also an increasing number of people who are prepared to do what it takes to achieve that goal.

There are those who are prepared to change their minds, their hearts and their circumstances in order to change the world in which they live and the picture in which they take part. They accept the view that man is evolving into an entirely new entity and that the earth is becoming aware of itself in a new way, so that energetically it is able to accommodate comfortably this new humanity.

WALKING THE TALK

People of earth should be reminded that they could be faced with an impossible situation as far as rape of the planet is concerned. Earth will fight back even more than it is doing already. Believe it or not, the mounting desecration and rape of the earth has an immediate correlation to the increasing incidence of paedophilia, rape and incest that is currently blighting the lives of so many people on earth.

It is the same for earth herself. There is such rape and pillage and destructive behaviour happening to the planet that earth will be forced to take revenge – as it is already doing. And in that revenge, innocent children will be the victims once again.

Earth is ready for the fight right now; because there is only so much pressure it can take on its resources. And by resources, we mean the rape of the inner sanctity of a sensuous being: as sensuous as any human being, and far greater in scope. What earth needs now is a break from that pressure and the voice of her protest is being heard as we speak.

Earth herself is a living, sentient, rewarding creature, alive to the sound of the music of the spheres. The more she is raped, the more she opens up to the idea that the spiritualising of matter is the only way to save her. When those of Light-heartedness walk on the earth, they help the earth remember who she is, and the urgency of knowing herself as part of a great chain of newly spiritualised dimensions.

Like all individuals, the earth needs to grow up, in the certainty of being of great merit and beauty. It is for those who walk on earth in the Light of heart to walk with intent. If they walk the path of heart, and in the Light of consciousness, they can know they are playing their part in bringing Light to the earth. Simply by walking their talk and becoming ambassadors of Light for the benefit of the earth herself, their lives have meaning.

Many of those who have the task of walking their talk for the Light of the World have been waiting in the wings for many years. There are some who have waited many lifetimes to begin their real work for planet earth. Lifetimes and lifetimes have been spent gathering experience; going through the highs ands lows of human history in order to gather strength – and Light – for the task they have committed to, since the beginning of Time itself. It is their time now.

Their task is to teach the world – at this time of collective transition from childhood to adulthood – how to make that transition with the least possible injury, both to themselves and the planet. And it is time now for humanity to listen. Not only to those people who have come here as ambassadors of Light, but also to the stirrings of earth as she also becomes conscious of herself as a Being of Light. It is time to listen to the music of the spheres, to the heavens breathing into conscious life within the heart of matter.

This may sound crazy and, indeed, at some level it is. And yet there are stirrings in every man and woman's heart now. Through the shaking up that has taken place; the failures and vicissitudes of globalisation; through the vast arena of global communication and global nightmare scenarios, we have been shocked out of our complacency sufficiently to make us feel that there has to be another way for human beings to exist on planet earth.

Those who are stirred are asking for guidance from those who they see carrying Light for the purpose. For those of Light-mindedness it is time to open up because there is nothing to lose now. They can be seen as light, yet know they are anchored safely on earth. They can, at last, offer themselves up to the task of guiding others to the heart of Light. They are no longer part of a karmic history that tells them they are unseen, unattractive and unlovable.

For now the human history of woundedness is a thing of the past. There is no woundedness in the dimensions that those of light travel in now. All they have to do is raise their game, raise their belief, raise their heads above the parapet and see themselves in their true light. This is a clarion call to those of like mind to trust the success of the journeys they have been on, trust they are carriers of beauty and light, and simply *be* in and of themselves, to themselves and to others, no matter how often the 'smaller picture' of their lives belies this truth.

All those of Light-mindedness are certainly now ready to become the leaders of men and women of heart who wish to change their minds, their lives and their circumstances, in order to follow their own inner hearts. Those of Light-mindedness are asked to teach by example, love by example and allow themselves to open up their environments to the new energy of loving kindness. Stop wondering what you are doing, whether what you are doing is right, and who will notice it anyway.

Even the established leaders of our society are questioning themselves right now; questioning their motives and their capacity to really understand human nature. Those of Light have much to give because they do understand human nature; they do understand the way the world is turning. They are needed now, whatever their doubts, to open up the way to others.

Our task is to help you do that, keep you on track, give you encouragement when the world is darker than seems possible, just at this stage when you are so ready to move forward into this light of time immemorial. Why not take this opportunity to take our hands; feel that you are amongst friends and let us all take this opportunity together to change the world.

RAGING EARTH

The most important thing to remember at this time is the Commandment, *'Thou shalt not kill'*. There is a great blood lust in humanity that needs to be assuaged in a completely different way at this time. There is anger, deep anger; there is suspicion, deep suspicion, and we need humanity to understand the causes of this primal need to shed blood, no matter how civilised man thinks he has become.

That is why the idea of the hunt, for example, is so intrinsically part of the lives of people of the earth: the farmers, the huntsmen, and those people closest to the natural world. And why in soldiery there is a determination in man to give his life for his country. And, more recently, the frenzy of knife crime as a way of giving vent to frustrations.

In fact it is the primal earth itself that has called for the spilling of blood. And within the deepest, primal nature of man the demands of earth are still strong. This demand for blood was nature's way, earth's way, of expressing her original anger at the prospect of God's spirit infiltrating the hallowed ground of matter, through the agency of man. Earth did not want man.

Time was of the essence for the descent of spirit into matter. 'The sons of God came down to mate with the daughters of men'. The 'aliens' came down to merge with the earth, but the earth fought back, in anger, by demanding that humanity fight for its life. The earth was lonely but mankind was nonetheless unwelcome: in the same way a lonely man does not want to be held to ransom by people better off than himself.

However, the old call of the unconscious can now be released. The earth, through man's understanding, can know that the 'aliens' came to integrate not to conquer. Man, whose task it is to be the instrument of the spiritualising of matter, is no longer called to fight, but to open up to peace.

Earth herself is now beginning to understand – through the auspices of those who are working on consciousness – that the 'invasion' of spirit was a *good thing*, and that man himself can now release that awful call for blood within his being. The earth can know that it is mankind's task to aid the earth and for earth to aid mankind. That it is a two-way energy flow of protectiveness and loving kindness.

The angry men of matter (who we see reaching a crescendo of rage, and releasing their unconscious urges in war, on women, on children, in the workplace, in society) can see it for what it is: the unconscious demand of the Old Order. They can release with dignity this hold the primal earth has had on them. Man no longer needs to express this raging torrent of abuse, neglect, despair and unhappiness. At the dawn of this new age, it is possible to bring peace to the human heart.

War is not a 'now' thing. War is a sign of the old order. Peace can reign on earth. We can see that moods, emotions, anger, despair, are the call of the primal in man. Man has been playing out this primal role through the rhythms and cycles of the old order, dictated by earth herself. No one is free to make choices in this primal soup of matter. Reactive behaviour borne out of instinct has no chance of freedom.

But man can now free himself to make his own choices. Freedom comes with consciousness, and the understanding that freedom is the result of spirit integrated into matter. This ultimately is the only way we are free to make personal choices. Releasing these primal moods and rages and urges, leads to awareness of the incoming spirit and thus to freedom of choice: choice for a new grace of movement and the pleasure of a new, emergent understanding.

Peace is possible without denying you a vibrant, creative output. In fact, peace is the perfect companion to creativity. Peace has a buzz within it: of action, of possibility, of real joy and personal achievement. How is that, when peace seems such a boring prospect, when you are geared up to war?

Peace has within it the most beautiful action of all. The action of loving kindness and out of that loving kindness comes the most glorious ability to act on others' behalf, not only in your own interests. Through peace comes action of the kind to which most people think they would like to become accustomed, but rarely achieve, because in the end it is me, me, me who is the most important person on planet earth.

Why is that? Why is 'me' so important do you think? When you act out of primal instincts, 'me' is the only one who can help you survive the vagaries and uncertainties of the old world order. Fighting one's own corner is the primal response to the uncertainties of being alive in a hostile world. Men may have fought for their womenfolk in the past, taken responsibility to feed and clothe them, but at what cost to women? At the cost of being held inferior, and thus comes more fear, more uncertainty, and often more dislike and anger between women and men.

But in a world infused by spirit, there is no fear and no uncertainty. In that place of peace you are held and you know you are held; you can feel you are held in the deepest sense of safety. This experience of peace cannot be talked about, it cannot be explained. It is simply 'the peace that passes all understanding'. This sense of peace and safety is the new inheritance that man can bring to planet earth. It is his by right and his to bring to fruition at this time of great fear and uncertainty.

Often it is the fear of losing the familiar and habitual – however unsatisfactory or painful that is – and the fear of boredom after lifetimes of 'drama' – however detrimental that drama has been – that brings fear of change. Consciously or unconsciously we fear even more what it might entail to be different.

It is the status quo, the primal need for 'fight and flight', which has kept men meaningfully employed since the beginning of time. But now, right now, it is time to change and time to let go of fear. It is time to allow the changes that are happening anyway, to happen; time to usher in the era of peace and understanding.

It is also the time of reckoning for those who wish to be ambassadors of Light, to open themselves up to a new sense of humanity in a peaceable world of individuals. By trusting that in choosing on behalf of the whole, they choose the best for themselves too, they can create individually and choose individually.

Of course this takes time; of course this takes risk, but underlying it all is the knowledge that you live in peace, you live in understanding, and that you are held; you are safe; you are loved.

BY THEIR FRUITS

The most significant aspect of greed is the assumption that one person is superior to another; in the sense that one person has more right to what is available than another person. In fact, everything that is happening now in the world, is the culmination of this attitude of supremacy of one person over another; whether it is white superior to black, or man superior to woman, or man superior to animals.

What began as neutral – the dualistic, paradoxical nature of humanity – became a lop-sided assumption of one side of the polarity 'ruling by right', which then repeated itself eon after eon, as the conquest of one side over the other.

Men became more and more aggressive, while women – or the feminine or negative polarity – became less and less aggressive. Greed is the result of man and woman, black and white, dominant and servile fighting for supremacy.

Knowing our place in society has changed little in essence over the ages, invariably registered by one side of a duality ruling over another. Whether that means one person having more sheep than another, or more education than another, or more white skin than another. In recent times, workers have fought bosses; women have fought men; Jews have fought Arabs, white men have fought Indians. And these fights that have brought into focus the level of greed that has reached this current apotheosis of negative aspiration.

It is time for the tables to turn now, for the world to let go this assumption that any one aspect of the duality is supreme over another. The spiritual aspiration of integrity, and the wish to integrate man's duality, is truly lapping at our heels. The old order of dominance and servility is sounding extremely shallow to our ears.

The world is becoming spiritualised more quickly than the most ardently religious could ever imagine. But this emergence is no longer about religion; it is about knowing the spirit of the universe we live in, and its descent into matter. It is the understanding that the duality that has defined mankind until now is moving towards integration and the spiritualising of man on earth.

Men and women can no longer be judged one way or the other for their supremacy or inferiority; their place in the hierarchy of dominance or servility; victor or victim. The winner, in the old sense, will not take all. Indeed it takes little imagination to see that the fittest are no longer surviving. It is the fittest that are falling, losing face, at this time.

The denying of God, the denial of a guiding force, the denial of a universal mandate that man is spirit as well as matter, is now no longer an option. What is emerging, whether obvious or not, is a completely new value system. It will no longer be a question of the fittest against the unfit, no longer antagonism between black and white, banker or worker. Each individual will come to recognise himself simply as a human being, who has come to earth at this time to promote a new dawn of a new age, each according to their own light.

From now on we judge not by who has most, but by the fruits that each generation is committed to offering to the sum of mankind. We can be seen as equals, simply expressing differently, by our individual light, the spiritual in matter.

We are at the dawn of an era in which each generation will open itself up to the energy of spirit that is appropriate to their age and appropriate to the age in which they are born. The wounds and insecurities that have accumulated through 'survival of the fittest' will be truly cleansed in the chaotic burnout that is happening at this time.

And yet, already, there are many people who have got the message, who simply cannot understand the current world view. The divisive measurement for who is who is alien to these enlightened souls. The idea that if you have money you have status; if you have celebrity you have something more to offer than those who do not.

These people are in every age group and every generation and yet they are exceedingly different one to the other. They have different tasks and different understandings of the magnificent, multidimensional world we inhabit and their place within it. Often they struggle with confusion about how they fit into the gross material world, particularly now it is exploding around them.

There are special children being born, for whom the fear of moving out into the world is too great. So they arrive 'walled up'. There are increasing numbers of dyslexics, children with

Aspergers syndrome or autism, and others who are sickly when they are very young. These 'children of the universe' often seem weak because they cannot function well in the old way. In fact, their strength lies in their difference, in their unusual perceptions, in their sense that this gross world is too hideous for them at times.

Also in the world today are many older people who are beginning to find and know their place. Not because they are the fittest, but because they are the most secure in who and what they are – living ordinary lives as spiritualised beings in human form.

These people exist independently within their own auric field, knowing they are different from those who yearn to be the fittest, the richest, and the most influential. They live 'anarchically', with integrity and self-responsibility. They know they are hugely influential simply because they are 'whole' people, in the right place, at the right time, in the right environment. So there are many people now available to propagate the vast change of emphasis in understanding what it is to be human.

TIME TO REFLECT

All who need to know themselves will know themselves in a very short time. Change is happening, and that change is happening fast. Be ready to take the plunge into the new and stand aside from the madness of the modern world. Step off the travelator that is taking you somewhere you do not want to go. Intrinsically you will know how much you want to get off the roller-coaster – thrilling as it might have been – because you have felt slightly sick and over-anxious, too many times.

Stop for a moment. Reflect on who you have become and what you have been doing: to yourself, to your family, to your friends and your 'underlings'. There has been such a separation of values from reality in recent times. So begin to think again, slowly and properly, about the consequences of your actions in, say, the past nine months. Sit down quietly and reflect. Light a candle, prepare your cup of tea or coffee and take time out, to think clearly about all you are, all you survey and all you have become.

It is guaranteed that everything is up for grabs now. Everything can be realigned; everything can be reassessed in the light of self and others. Why not begin with your child, your partner, your cat, your workmate. Is there anything that could be changed in that relationship? Is that relationship appropriate for you own well-being, and consequently for their well-being? Be tough on yourself; be honest, be truthful.

If you meditate on each relationship you have, ponder clearly on it inside your being; you will feel intuitively what has been wrong, what is inappropriate, what needs to change.

Once you begin to register the 'wrongness' in relating, then you can begin to open up to the wrongness of parts of your life; see which parts are not serving you well, and consequently not serving your environment well. Slowly, slowly it will dawn on you, what and who is best for you, and in the long run best for them. The anxieties can subside; the intensity of the emotion in your life can wither on the vine. Only the most truthful, the most appropriate, the most beautiful, the most wise need remain.

Consider the birds in the trees, the lambs in the fields, the time you have wasted on fatuous pursuits. Think 'different', think change, think loving kindness and all will emerge, all will manifest in a new truth, a new day, a new dawn. Feel the colour return to your life. The highs and lows subside but the vividness remains clear and candid. Open yourself up to the beauty of tasks that bring joy and pleasure, not anxiety and indecision. What are you doing, where are you going, who are you now?

We are waiting with baited breath to welcome those of you who do decide to take on your full humanity at this time. There is every chance that all those who wish to join forces with the delights of the universe will become aware of the vast occasion and great opportunity that is now.

All of us who wait are the millions of souls who have been

preparing for this moment of change; who have predicted through the ages that there will come a time when mankind opens up its heart to the sense of the universe as a living, breathing whole. You are the one who can make this choice. You are the one who can recognise that you are the star of your own life, and a star of universal significance on planet earth.

How does this work?

The universe is a mine of information. Information, we know, is the currency of the present day, the currency of the techno-logical era. But the true significance of this technological revolution is that it parallels what is happening in the universe. Within cyberspace are layers and layers and layers of information just waiting to be tapped. Not through machines; not through computers, iPods, or other machinations of technological thought, but through the human body, through the human mind, through the human heart.

There is no place like home. Begin by being at home in your own body. Allow yourself the privilege of knowing that you can tap into the stars simply by using the most refined technological instrument there has ever been: the human body itself.

Yes, the human being is evolving, is being prepared – through the auspices of universal loving kindness – to reach the stars without the need for rocket science, but through a deep resonance of understanding and experience within the human framework itself.

Think about that. You yourself are all you need. You are the instrument of your own understanding. You are the great 'I am' of the universe. Within your own being is all you need to become aware of, and be instrumental in, the understanding that the universe is a living, breathing, mighty network of information in cyberspace.

When we say the human body we mean the human body; the spiritual ideal embedded in matter. This does not mean behaving like a lunatic bat, flying around your own head, with sonic location to keep you flying high, which is what drugs achieve. Drugs hike you out of your body so you buzz about like a manic bat picking up resonances of a disembodied kind, which can ultimately drive you mad.

No, what you are seeking through the human body is a deep link to the Divine within your own nature.

The deepest resonance of safety, peace and understanding, comes through hard work. It comes through the efforts you make to keep yourself away from the emotional Ferris wheel that is determined to take you for a ride, and keep you insecure, unhappy and anxious. This does not require you to sit on a mountaintop, chanting for God presence. It means living, breathing, working in the world of men and women, in simplicity, in gratitude, in loving embrace with all you survey.

And as you are able more and more to live in this state of grace, so you see more clearly, love more dearly and open up more nearly to God presence, in the form of all his creatures; those nearby on earth, and those far away in the universal system of loving kindness.

THINK SMALL, THINK LESS

It is important to consider the following for the enhancement of humanity:

There does need to be management of the number of people on planet earth before all men can be fed. Which does mean that there needs to be a new understanding that man cannot continue to breed unthinkingly, as it has since time immemorial. By this we mean that people have many children when their lives are about survival and feeding themselves into old age.

Unsustainable growth on every level has been the norm since time began and that includes unsustainable growth of the numbers of people on planet earth. While humanity thinks that 'growth' is the ideal and the only criterion for life on earth, then growth on every level will be seen as desirable.

Yet cancer, for example, is the outcome and display of uncontrollable growth, and it is now the scourge of the age. And while cancer parallels the way man lives, in an uncontrollable growth environment, cancer will continue to be the indictment of this way of thinking.

When man thinks 'sustainable', 'small', 'simple', there will be enough for everyone on planet earth, and the current, innate, addictive need to 'grow' will become a thing of the past. It will be the understanding of natural growth, not primal greed that enters men's hearts and minds. There will not be too many children, or the addiction to growth, or uncontrollable levels of cancer.

Addictive behaviour will become a thing of the past. Addiction is the mechanism by which people determine to fill the emptiness, conscious or unconscious, they feel in their lives. It is the way they try to plug the great big gap they experience inside – until it gets out of control.

There is less anxiety when growth is controlled. There is less neediness – emotionally, physically and mentally – when we stop being driven by the need to have, and have, and have again. Nature's way is for energy to follow thought. And once our addiction to growth subsides, so man will reduce in numbers, enabling the living, breathing planet to sustain its people in loving kindness.

Having children will simply be part of nature's way of replenishment, not an inalienable right as it seems to have become in recent times. It is the primal in man that dictates so many of the addictions we have today, including this strongest drive of all – to procreate.

When man 'grows up' nature will take its course in a way that human beings will be happy to co-operate with. Children will once again come naturally. The increase in sterility today, is nature's way of closing down the endless growth of humanity. Our arrogance in growing children on demand is bringing more and more chaos to earth. Earth can no longer support this rampant demand for more.

Man is not omnipotent – as we are constantly reminded – despite his continuing attempts to be so. Darwin's 'survival of the fittest' supports the supremacy of our primal urge, which demands we survive at all costs. The gene, they contend, is omnipotent. And yet, as Nature becomes more and more imbued with spirit, with the Divine, and with the finer arts in man through human consciousness, we see that it is not. Ignore that at your peril.

It is the spirit that continues forever, and humanity now has the opportunity to know itself in Life Everlasting. If we allow in the magnitude of spirit and all that this contains, we can know ourselves, once and for all, as more than just our genes.

HAPPINESS

Every human being has a wish to be happy in life. Sometimes taking drugs allows a person to be happy for a fleeting moment. And when that seems so rare in normal life, the promise of even that fleeting moment is enough to become addictive. But taking drugs to be happy always brings diminishing returns, and more of the drug is needed each time, to reach that fleeting state of happiness you crave.

Why is happiness so elusive for human beings at this time?

It is because of our increasing need to be in a high state of glamour and drama: there are such high stakes now. The speed of communication allows us to see what is happening in every part of the world, and we yearn for what we imagine it takes us to be happy: we demand more food, more drugs, and generally more consumption. Happiness in the modern world is based it seems, purely and simply on greed. But this will never bring happiness, only the demand for more and more 'having'.

Happiness is elusive because our basic premise about happiness is wrong. Happiness is something to be savoured; to be tasted; to be tested, as an interior effect, not grabbed, or yearned for, or given of right by the exterior world. Happiness is an inner experience for those of integrity, of deserving; who accept with fortitude the meaning of the vagaries and beauty of life, and live that with truth and meaning.

Happiness comes through understanding, through being of use to mankind and, most of all, simply by being. It means taking those steps, moment by moment, in faith and trust, into the arena of happiness that mankind has been promised: Life Everlasting on earth.

Happiness is the by-product of simplicity, kindness, and respect for all other beings. Happiness is not the result of 'having', in the accepted sense. In many ways it is the result of 'not having'. Inner clarity, richness of inner understanding, and the joy and pleasure of simplicity and contentment, are not things you 'own', but rather the state of being in which you live.

Happiness sings inside you when there is harmony of spirit and matter. The true test of happiness is when all feels complete and whole. Happiness is being in love with Life itself. And Life is the key to all you survey. Life itself holds the deepest meaning of who you are, and what it is to be alive in this century, in this moment, in this way, in this understanding – because Life itself is only now becoming conscious of itself on planet earth.

LIFE BREATHES INTO LIFE

The Life Force is becoming conscious of its own nature in a way that it has never done before. The Life Force is the engine of Life; the beginning and end of everything that has ever been and ever shall be on planet earth. The Life Force is waking up to cognition that it is the engine of Life Everlasting; that it is the replica, the mirror image of Life Everlasting on earth. It is the 'inner sanctity' of everything that ever was and ever shall be.

What is meant by 'the inner sanctity' of everything that ever was and ever shall be?

The Life Force has become the cognition factor for all that exists on earth at this time. Planet earth is the means by which the universe and Life Everlasting knows itself to exist. In other words, it is the Life Force becoming conscious of itself that allows us to know Life Everlasting as a tangible reality; to know that we are and ever shall be, in this world and the next.

Is this leaving you breathless?

We do hope so. Because then and only then will you become aware of how important the breath is to the human being, to the planet as a whole and to the universe, and to Life Everlasting.

Breath is the engine of the soul, and the soul is the engine of the Life Force, and the Life Force is the engine of Life Everlasting. And so, to be aware of the value and importance of breathing is number one priority for mankind. To breathe properly and fully, with dignity and decision, is to begin to become aware, at the very deepest level, of all that is man; that is God and Life and Love.

Breathing with consciousness is more important than anything else at this time. No one breathes properly: with purpose, and understanding. All too many people breathe with such shallowness that they are lifted out of body as surely as drug takers are lifted out of body.

Believe it or not, we are so keen not to be alive, not to be present in our own bodies and in our own lives, that we will do anything we can to raise ourselves off the planet. We crave to live out of body, outside the scope of real truth – the truth that when we are fully embodied we are spiritual beings, and as such can attain Life Everlasting while still on earth.

Within the human being is a death wish. It is part of the paradoxical matter of being alive; with as much a wish to die as there is to be alive. The 'death wish', though, is unconscious; the underbelly of what it is to be human in a human body. Unconsciously we yearn to 'die', to join with the spirit outside the body in 'heaven'. And we live, for the most part, wandering half outside the body, unconsciously searching for our 'lost soul'.

This is true. Human beings unknowingly wish to exist outside the human framework, and their yearning for 'more' is becoming increasingly insistent now. The trouble is they mistakenly think that this yearning can be assuaged through acquiring more and more 'stuff'. In fact what they really need and are searching and yearning for, is something far more meaningful, far more interiorly satisfying. The urgency is coming from the need to feel whole again.

The antidote to this 'unrequited love' must begin within the body itself; coming back to basics, back to the awareness that most of our time we spend 'out of body'. So the best thing we can do is to come back down to earth.

By being fully embodied we can begin to understand our emptiness, our yearning in a more realistic way. We can build up confidence again and release the fear of being on the outside in an alien world, which so many people feel. We can agree to join the human race in the way it is meant to be at this time. We can begin to recognise ourselves as the most beautiful and fulfilled creatures, richly endowed with warmth and kindness and inclusiveness.

The world is ready to be embodied again. It is time to breathe fully. It is time to breathe in the beautiful air of consciousness that brings us down to earth; that eases us down inside our bodies where everything we need exists. It is time to take a breather from the fears and anxieties of being suspended above the earth, looking in with envy.

HELPING YOURSELF

Most people do not know they are floating three feet above the earth in 'no man's land', unable to be in touch with earth in a full and wholesome way, and certainly not in touch with spirit. They may be able to contact parts of themselves that have floated off into the ethers since time immemorial, aspects of themselves that could not cope with the realities of incarnation. They may even experience this dislocation as a psychic ability. But this is not truth.

The truth is that they prefer, unknowingly, to stay in no man's land, neither here nor there, for most of their lives, possibly living on the glamour of the psychic, rather than face their own fears head on.

There are many competent therapies that can help bring those elusive parts back into line, to urge you into true alignment with yourself, on earth. There are therapies to soothe the anxieties, to show you emotional equilibrium, to bring you down to earth.

If you choose your practitioner wisely, therapies can offer you the opportunity to understand the reasons behind your isolation and pain. It is time to take these opportunities and work diligently with what they have to offer. For now is an ideal time to bring through to consciousness a rich seam of creativity that is completely independent of the highly charged wounds and dramas of your personal and collective past.

No more drama is the order of the day. No more flare-ups of major proportions, inner or outer, each time you perceive a hurt, hear a slight, or imagine a misunderstanding. Let go the desire for histrionics when someone else is taking your limelight. Allow the world to turn in a calm and rational way.

Few people are emotionally detached and rational, however much they perceive and deceive themselves to the contrary. All they are doing is rationalising their defensive behaviour as normal.

Normal human behaviour does not reach out to wound, to rebel, to hurt, to seek revenge. Normal behaviour – in this new day of this new dawn – sees Life itself as the reason for living, not revenge or anger or feeling superior. Life is magical; Life is clever; Life has every trick up its sleeve to make you happy and content, creative and well-nourished. If only human beings were not so determined to continue fighting for their lives, but could just let go and Live for their lives.

SLOWING DOWN

Our task today is to make the bridge between the gods and humanity at a time of great excitement in the heavens. Man is coming of age, and in this moment there is a high state of interest in the fate of mankind, as we know it.

There are always glitches in the heavens: times when things do not go according to plan. Yes, mistakes are made and the plan goes awry for a moment in time – eons of time, perhaps, in the human experience of space-time – but less than an instant in our framework of understanding.

So there is an opportunity at this moment in time for the world to come back on track. This needs to happen so the heavens, too, can move on to a new and exalted level of under-standing. The universe must know itself as the backdrop in which God's loving kindness becomes the engine of movement throughout all the solar systems of infinity.

This is D-Day: the time when the mighty forces of loving kindness come storming up the beaches of humanity, in order to dispel the 'occupation' by the dark forces once and for all.

The dark forces, as we have indicated throughout this work, are the basic, historic insecurities of mankind that have lead to acts of evil, revenge, hate, suspicion, and unconscionable compet-itive strategies – all based on the 'first fear' that God did not love his own creation and threw him out of heaven. Primal, uncon-scious fear is the basis of all the negativity on planet earth and letting go of fear is the one true goal for mankind at this time. It is time to feel once again that 'the hand of God' is a loving, supportive hand, of a merciful God who does not judge.

Everyone in incarnation at this time can take this step to salvation; of course they can. But it will take commitment. And there are those who will never wish to make that commitment because life is too exciting in the 'fast lane' – the fast lane, which reaches a dead end, of course.

Why is that? The fast lane requires a great deal of energy to maintain. We call that energy adrenalin. Adrenalin can only last so long, go so far; it is like the fuel in a motorcar; eventually it will run out. Think of all those burnt-out people as they pile up at the end of the lane. In their thirties, forties, fifties they have already run out of gas. Surely it makes sense, in this age of ecological awareness, to use our personal energy more wisely too.

Adrenalin, this fuel of life, also crashes out through anxiety. And anxiety is the main cause of all the chronic illnesses we have to face, at an earlier and earlier age. Chronic illness is caused by the stress and anxiety we place on ourselves at every turn: when we feel we do not match up; when we feel defensive and insecure, and especially when we know we'll never make the fast lane but keep trying all the same.

The fast lane is where the crashes happen: pile-up upon pile-up. And they are happening more and more as the fast lane becomes congested with the 'haves', and the 'have-nots' who wish that they had. The niggling aches and pains that adrenalin junkies suffer are getting worse and worse, and at a younger and younger age. The world is becoming sick and tired through life in the fast lane.

Why not take a break and renew your energy. Refresh your body; drink in the Life Force that is waiting to power you in a cleaner, purer, more effective and more wonderful way. Adrenalin junkies feed off fear and excitement and restlessness and yet, in time, the restless will become sick. It is as simple as that.

Flu bugs are drawn to restlessness. There is an excitement, a fever in the virus community, a restlessness to grow and mutate and dig their heels in. They alight on restlessness; they thrive in the fast lane. Think about that. Viruses want to grab on to the excitement of the fast pace of modern living. They are in for the ride and love it sufficiently to mutate and mutate and mutate. So stop worrying, stop the world and they will get off!

MINDING YOUR OWN BUSINESS

The world turns in mysterious ways and certainly not in the ways most people think it does. Politicians speak empty words now, so why should they know better than you do what is best for the whole? Man is coming of age in order to make his own choices, know his own mind and allow consensus to rule. Consensus rule is the only way to go now.

Why should you not feel powerful? There is little to recommend the kind of power that exists in the hands of those who would wish to have power today. There is little to recommend the current world view. So why not be powerful yourselves? Why not? But this power requires some careful consideration.

Power demands the integrity of understanding of what it is to be a spiritualised human being in a changing world. It asks for a new kind of responsibility for the decisions made on your own behalf and therefore on behalf of others. If you make a mistake about yourself, then you make a mistake on behalf of everyone else. We are all connected by threads so strong that you cannot swot a fly without that having repercussions in the universe.

In fact, as unloving as it sounds, it does not really matter about the flies. They do not belong to the new world view, or even to the old world view. They are the dinosaurs of the current age and must disappear in the next few hundred years. Flies are the busybodies of the planet, and 'busybodying' is not something to be recommended for planet earth. Human busybodies are less concerned with their own lives than with interfering, according to their own needs and views, in the lives of other people.

And this is the point. Politicians have now become 'busybodies'. They think they can buzz around your head, telling you what to do, getting in your way, making life a misery with their noise and presence and interfering. They distract you from the purpose of your own integrity and make you feel anxious and frustrated. You long to swot them away from what you consider to be your own business.

Busybodying has become endemic in socialist governments and corruption has become endemic in totalitarian ones. These polarities have stretched so wide they have pushed themselves and us beyond endurance. A balancing mechanism has to come into play. Equally, and above all, individual human beings need to apply themselves to their own polarities, their own excesses. They must take themselves in hand and work towards personal integration and freedom.

Only then will the world be ready for consensual rule. When each individual is conscious, to the extent they can be, of their own integration, self-regulation, self-discipline and self-responsibility, they then deserve the wisdom to guide the general population at large.

Then the busybodies, who constantly fuss about others' behaviour but take very little account of their own, will be extinct. And we will choose with integrity those of integrity, to work on their own and others' behalf with integrity. Only then can we have the wisdom of consensual rule.

One tree cut down in the rain forest affects the weather in the rest of the world. If one man or woman works hard towards integrity, then the effects will radiate out into the whole universe. Where clouds of fear once blighted the world, so rainbows can lighten the sky.

THE PLAY CAN BEGIN

'All the world's a stage; the men and women merely players'. Mankind, at this time, is a people waiting in the wings of its own life. It is the moment before the show goes on, when everyone has stage fright before the performance of a lifetime. The first night is finally here. The players who have learned their lines,

who have fully understood the part they are about to play, will offer themselves up to the glory of the part and do their very best to shine.

And yet, it is the whole company that must shine if the performance is to be the success everyone is hoping for. We have been waiting for those who have had difficulty remembering their lines to catch up.

But now we are ready. We are primed to give and receive the play: full of promise, full of beauty, full of great actors playing their parts for the good of the company. Yet we also play for the good of the audience that has been waiting expectantly, to be thrilled, to be changed, to be brought into the action of this brilliantly executed play.

We, the audience, the co-conspirators, have been waiting to draw out the best from those in the thick of the action. It is we, the expectant audience that has willed the best from the performers, because we, the audience, are depending on them. It is up to the performers to use their skills and bring the excitement of transformation to those who are watching.

The universe waits with baited breath to be changed and enriched, to be moved and moved on, by the best performance possible of a new play performed by new mankind. Indeed, the dress rehearsals are over. The play is about to begin.

THE RETURN

Who are we? We are the Lords of Time who gave birth to the current universe. We gave you life; we gave you freedom to choose your path. And now you have come of age, you are ready to return us to ourselves. What goes out must come back: that is a law of the universe. A star expands until it implodes upon itself. This moment in human time is, in a manner of speaking, an implosion into the black hole of time. It is not the end of the world but a return to normality.

When life is hit by this returning energy, there is fear. It is disturbing not to expand, expand, expand. To contract and contract makes people nervous and angry. Everything on earth is expected to happen in tune with an expanding universe. When there is the inner sense that there is nowhere else to expand to, we feel trapped and unhappy.

The experience of 'return' adds a new dimension to everything that has come before. Expansion is febrile but exciting, but for the moment, as the juggernaut turns round, life in the throes of the return is disappointing.

In the old world view, in an expanding universe, the influence of Pleiades was wholly significant. But as with all things taken to the limit of excess, that particular influence is already inappropriate. Runaway expansion, and the gizmos of expansion have turned life as we now know it into fantasy and will be cordoned off as a parallel reality. In the returning universe it is the energy of Sirius that can light upon humanity.

Many people feel out of alignment with the coming new world. Evolutionary change is marked through external means, so it is not surprising that there is widespread physical discomfort, disjointedness, structural pain and disability.

We can already see that this is a phenomenal time of change. We witness the slimming down or crashing out of overblown structures and more people who realise the inappropriateness of what they are doing are handing in their resignations. We are relieved when we hear truth from those who speak honestly about the reality of their lives. The great 'myth of power' is being blown away and exposed for what it truly is: just power.

For many people, though, the experience of the returning universe is indeed more comfortable. These are the individuals who finally feel at home, now that the wind is changing, and are pleased with the direction things are going. Until this moment they have felt displaced, and distressed by the constant demand to be more than they can be. They have been waiting on the shore for the tide to turn.

It is they who are now on the rising tide, and can lead others forward. Not to a bigger, better, louder, more manic world, but towards a minimalist, less dramatic, yet more effective and qualitative life.

This is not an iron framework, like the old world view where one size fits all and causes suffering and difficulty for those who do not fit the frame. It is a creative opportunity to be more free, less needy and in tune with God.

A CHANGE OF HEART

Everything is in a state of flux. All the birds, bees, animals and insects are feeling a strange nerviness in the environment, just as every human being, to a greater or lesser extent, is feeling unnerved. For all the realms on earth are in the process of a tremendous change of heart.

It is this change of heart that brings a sense of nerviness in the air. And this feeling of dis-ease and disjointedness is the cause of so much death and destruction in the animal kingdom, as well as in the human kingdom. Varroa in bees, TB in cattle, and the destruction of insects by insects is happening because of this disturbance in the environment. Of course there is man-made destruction, too, but the effect of these disturbances comes more from the inner planes than the outer. Why not accept that.

But a change in man's behaviour cannot come about through namby-pamby rules and regulations, by simply legislating for every aspect of human behaviour. This transition into a new world view must come through understanding, by teaching people the inner workings of man and beast now.

There is edginess and tension in the air. It is an 'in-between' moment when everyone feels edgy and out of sorts from time to time. This provokes actions and reactions, dissatisfactions and repercussions, and the strong are tempted to tyrannise the weak in order to ease their tensions. Edginess is like addiction and for some requires extreme acts to release their pent-up feelings.

But this edginess will pass soon enough. Once again there will be calm in the firmament and a tangible sense of release will be felt throughout the planet. The time will come when we can really catch up with ourselves. We will love the prospect of a simpler life, a truer life, and a longer, healthier life. We will no longer feel a sense of dread, but experience ourselves stretching into infinity, every moment of the day.

Infinity is the experience of the New Jerusalem, of each individual belonging to a vast creation of man-made and heaven-sent life on earth. Old Jerusalem has symbolised a world endlessly fought and cried over, separated and twisted to mean something different to each division of religious fervour. But New Jerusalem will belong to you – and me – in equal measure. My Jerusalem is my Jerusalem, but your Jerusalem is yours. The crusading, the jihading will stop: one view over another, one 'righteousness' over another will cease.

In twenty years' time, no one will feel the same as they do today. When Pluto enters the sign of Aquarius astrologically: when all the old structures, inner and outer, are broken down – as described by Pluto's current journey through the sign of Capricorn – then will come the true Age of Aquarius. It heralds an age of true learning, a time of true community and true companionship, formed in a clean and detached way and separated from the emotional debilitations of the old order.

Twenty years for the edginess to stop and a further twenty years to begin to learn how to live with one another in a land of plenty, detached from the 'awe-fullness' of one race over another. Then humanity can move on, towards an era of huge creative output and exploration: to know the true meaning of what it is to be a cog in the wheel of mankind on a fully spiritualised earth.

ON BEING A STAR BEING

In the beginning, the *idea* of humanity was to realign to the heavenly bodies in the Milky Way. But now mankind is ready to recreate the Milky Way on earth. Millions of people on the planet at this time are being asked to become their 'star selves' in this current incarnation. Individuals are finding themselves pulling away from tribal allegiances – whether this is the larger tribe or the family tribe – in order to become 'star beings'.

There are many people here on earth who have worked quietly but consciously – some for their whole lives – to individualise. Actively or loosely they consider themselves part of the growing 'subculture': the 'growth movement' or 'new age' or adherents of 'mind, body and spirit'. Or simply know, from their own experience, that there is a greater meaning to life.

To strive for 'individuation' is the starting point for the withdrawal from tribal, family, and even couple culture, which demand our co-dependency and keep us infantilised. As we individuate and separate, and invite in the intimacy of spirit, so a light system of individual stars is being released into earth's atmosphere, forming a network of light. Slowly the earth is being released from the bondage of man's unredeemed narcissism, becoming more compatible for the arrival of more star beings.

There are also those in this subculture who have understood intellectually what they are being asked to do, but can only now begin to trust sufficiently and accept the separation. It takes such courage to risk living the truth of a star being. It takes courage to face the realisation of just how great and just how separate we are in the world, and how okay that is.

Where humanity as a whole has fought hard to 'belong', a star being trusts the planet and the process. He knows himself to be separate, without fear or worry that he is alone. He knows he is held and supported by a vast network of universal loving kindness. Only when we reach this level of separation and trust, do we realise how dependent we have been on others; how much drama we have created in our lives in order to feel safe and alive.

The process of individuation means looking at the past and the present and leaving behind the hang-ups and imprints that have become the guiding principles of our lives. It means letting go the past events and situations that have insistently demanded certain attitudes and behaviours, and been transferred over many lifetimes.

In this lifetime we must cut the umbilical cord from mother, release the influence of father and brother and sister. In this process we can see the meaning of the lessons we have learned, and then leave our history behind. Losing the 'baggage' is like free-fall without a parachute, but once we have landed on earth we realise that this is where safety reigns.

It is a lonely furrow to plough. Yet it is the only way to know fully what it means to be here on earth: to be present in the now moment, and to know – somewhere deep down – that you know what you are meant to be doing. Being human has always been so difficult; but with your feet on the ground comes a sense of true independence and 'self-referencing'.

So, what is the difference between this experience of self-referencing and the narcissism of your life before?

Before 'self-referencing' you were centre stage with all the people in your life acting in your drama. Friends, family and acquaintances were actively engaged in your story, the characters pulled on and off stage, as required, to make the scenario work.

But having landed, there is no stage and it feels as though no one else is around in the same way with the same purpose. You are still in relationships, intimate and otherwise, but, in truth, they feel different. You are fully present but somehow on your own. And you know where and what you need to be, in order to fit safely and comfortably into your own skin. You want simply to express the richness of who you are, however that may be: in nature; in the art studio; in a social or business context, or by baking cakes, or being a parent.

The key to being a star being on planet earth is achieving a sense of separation and safety and a love of being on earth. It does not mean being all-powerful, all glorious; but nonetheless feels determined and influential.

It is time for a new kind of relating. 'Separation' prevents relationships from becoming sticky or upsetting or producing painful conflicts of interest. There is no longer need to be defensive or on the attack to make yourself safe, because the level of safety you wish for is in your own hands.

When there are other 'stars' around you, there is a real sense of delight, knowing you are a star in your own right. There is a feeling of being more alive, and a sense of pleasure that other stars are shining independently alongside you. It is easy to enjoy their company and act appropriately. Star beings can engage in a new and independent way, based on detached loving kindness. You can flow in your own river without getting caught up by the jagged stones.

RESONANCE NOT EMPATHY

This is the moment of truth, because it is difficult to filter out truth from non-truth at this time. Truth is absolute, and yet truth is absolute only in terms of how we each perceive it to be true. There is a new truth: a new beauty, a new understanding of truth and beauty within a new world view.

How do we distinguish truth from fiction? How do I distinguish my truth from your truth, and, more than that, my truth from wrong truth? These are the questions that tax people of integrity most at this time.

The only way to establish truth is to 'know yourself'. Know yourself so well that you know for yourself what is your truth and what is not your truth when you come amongst others in your environment. It is a listening process of true resonance.

Resonance is now the most important attribute coming to mankind and goes beyond empathy. Empathy is the best of the old order, the instrument by which the emotionally literate have experienced their environment in a truer, deeper and more individualised way. Empathy has been the glue that has drawn together like to like, metaphor to reality, and people of like mind and experience, in order to herald the journey to the path of resonance.

After separation and detachment from the old dramas of human interaction, resonance is the new tool for spiritual understanding. Resonance is the received wisdom of universal unfolding, after the integration of spirit and matter within each human being.

Resonance is the beautiful experience of one being resonating with another. It is as though one star resonates with another, rather than merges. Resonance, unlike empathy, does not affect the other adversely or change the other for better or worse.

The observer does not change the observed, as implied in quantum theory, but allows it to resonate freely and independently. Together they produce something bigger than they do individually.

It is interesting to see how the recent phenomenon of social networking has introduced and heightened the place of empathy into the techno environment. It allows us see quite plainly how empathy can change others for good, but can also be manipulative.

The world is changing rapidly through this incredible magnification. As technology speeds up the old order for yet more change, we must wait to see how this influences the newly unfolding process. When resonance, not empathy, becomes the engine of evolution, globalisation will come to mean a Milky Way of individualised and independent star beings existing in resonance.

The physics of matter and the cosmos will take a different direction. New scientific theories will be found for human evolution. There will be new theories about gravity, and those elusive particles will be seen through resonance not empathy. There will be advances and changes in biological thinking, as new elements, changed elements, are discovered that allow the body to function more suitably in resonance than empathy.

FIGHTING YOUR OWN SHADOW

In the meantime, how can we make a stand against the influx of negativity that bounces around us day after day? Why is it so difficult to stand strongly against the energies that bombard us from 'outer space', which in fact are our own negative energies fighting us back! The way to do this is to stop fighting: it's as simple as that. The world insists on fighting its own shadow. That is what all wars are: human beings fighting their own shadows.

People perceive slights and hurts and competitiveness from the outside, to the extent that these exist within themselves. Nations are no different from individual human beings. As we have said before, wars are fought because man insists on fighting his own inner demons and woundedness.

There is such a simple solution to this fighting and warring and drawing of blood, to the killing and maiming that has gone on since time immemorial and is still happening today in hysterical proportions. The answer, as an individual, is to stop fighting your shadow, and look instead at those hurts and slights and injuries sustained over lifetimes of hard-fought and hard-won experience.

'Stop the world I want to get off', for a moment. Take a look at why you are at war with yourself. Why you are always two people: the victim and the victor? And no matter how much you defend the one or the other, they still keep warring?

This is the duality of what it is to be human in this current stage of human evolution. But it is not for ever. We need not be forever at war with ourselves. The time is coming when the integration of opposites is possible. But you have to see it for yourselves: just how clever mankind is in journeying to soul consciousness and consciousness of the God in Self.

Why not sit down today and think it through. Why am I at

war with myself all the time? Why do I sit on the fence of my own life without digging down into the bowels of who I am? After all, what is life for if not to understand who and what you are?

You have the mind, the heart and the will to do it, so why not take a look at yourself. What else is worth all the effort of getting up in the morning and starting a new day? What else but the excitement and pleasure of knowing why you are here and why you are here with those you are here with. What is in it for me – and for him and her and everyone else on the planet? It is such an exciting time. Why waste it on war?

The task right now is to bring into our world view the modicum of intelligence that has been missing so far. This is the intelligence of understanding pattern, of understanding the meaning of the harmony of the spheres, so that humanity can look at itself in a different light. Literally.

A different light is being shed on humanity, a sort of infrared light that enables humanity to see itself in a different way. In the way you can see a fox in the dark with a special camera, you can now light up the darkness by opening up the portals of your history. We can help you see how it works, how you work, and how you can move forward into this light of Everlasting Love.

Many people are afraid to open up what they perceive as a 'can of worms'. They fear they are too bad, too guilty, too unlovable, to look themselves full in the face. But everyone is guilty, unpleasant, and even potentially evil in the baseness of their being. This is what it has meant to be human – to experience the full range of the duality in matter on planet earth.

When you are able to face the wrath of God, the fear of being judged by God, you can then move forward in peace. You can see that you have been your own worst enemy, your own worst taskmaster. You recognise yourself as the slave driver, the perse-cutor, and know that you elected to be the pawn in your own game, ultimately to experience and understand God's loving kindness on earth. And what is more, you understand the privilege of being part of the cohort currently in incarnation that is bringing the earth up to speed for universal change.

'SELF' CONSCIOUS

Everything that is happening now has been ordained since time immemorial. The details of the blueprint are often changed through vicarious routes, but the inexorable trend towards this moment has paradoxically been set since time began. Now, however, as the world turns, time takes on a different meaning for those who have understood the mechanisms of consciousness. The choices to be made for the future are left more and more to the individual conscience.

'Anarchy', however, is only safe in the hands of those with integrity, who are cognisant of what it is to be self-responsible, self-motivated, self-rewarding. The idea of 'Self' is still a confusing construct for most people. Self is the instruction kit you possess for bringing the very best outcome to planet earth. Self has so many components: you would not believe how many strands there are that make up self-confidence, self-enhancement and self-regulation.

That is why it has taken eons and eons for the emergence of the Self: that is, the sum total of what it takes collectively for humanity to become aware of itself. In earlier times, even those who proposed the edict 'Know Thyself', had no idea the extent of the evolving dimensions of the reality that make up the Self.

Now, however, there is truly the opportunity to know yourself. At this juncture, when time itself is changing course, the dimensional reality in which all the computations of Self are available to the human gaze, the Self can be fully known. Even the most ardent seeker after truth can be happy.

It is like an epiphany. After all those eons of seeking, it is as though it is now possible to experience infinity in one sweeping gaze, and in that precious moment, to understand 'it all'. 'It' can land wholly and simply into consciousness and human beings can know themselves as if for the very first time.

Truth can come upon us. We can now know truth and live in truth, simply by being human. Whereas in the past we have needed to die to know truth, and in that dying have continued through many, many lifetimes and died many, many times. It is in this incarnation, now, that we can gaze on truth as if for the first time.

Our task now is to help you forget time! Forgetting time is to allow yourself to fill up with Holy Spirit, however that is expressed for you within the individuality that you are now. You are happy to be an individual; happy to become the simplicity of what you are meant to be in this time of greed and anxiety. You are happy to know yourself as more than you could ever have imagined yourself to be.

And yet, there is also a new paradoxical truth: that you cannot become more than who you are. The new paradigm presents a new paradox: that there is limitation even in the world of the limitlessness of Life Everlasting. The scientists need to know, too, that you are limited in a limitless world. And those limitations, despite the incredible knowledge and experience that you live in an infinite world, will bring you all to your senses. Yes, your senses.

COMING TO OUR SENSES

Even though your senses are enhanced beyond measure when the limitless life of spirit comes into play inside the body, the senses are ultimately finite. That is why, despite bringing your God-self into being, you can never know God quite to the degree that satisfies you. In the beginning your senses are your means for clawing your way to God. But at a certain point you must know you have reached your peak. You can reach a peak of perfection in this life and then can you rest.

Yes, you can rest on your laurels. When you find you are

happy with what you have and who you are, then comes peace. The pendulum stops for a moment and the movement changes. Instead of inexorably moving forward towards an endless and impossible goal, you sit still, feeling richly endowed and full to the brim, radiating and resonating all that you are.

Because you have reached the fullness of what you can be in this lifetime, you know you are effective, beautiful, and rewarded enough. Your movement changes, your way through life changes, which brings a deep sense of commitment, contentment, and love for what you are, who you are and where you are going. You are as much 'it all' as you possibly can be, and that is enough.

The new children coming into this world cannot be rushed: they cannot be hurried through life, as government and parents might wish them to be. The new children will feel their way in a different way; make themselves felt in a different way. They will arrive on earth already rich and full within themselves and will not wish to hurtle through life at the current desperate speed. They will not want to 'have' and 'hold on to' in the same way as more recent generations.

Until they are five or six years of age these children will not respond to urging or cajoling to be like everyone else. They will wish to explore their inner resources, silently for the most part and eventually, knowing that who they are is enough, will act accordingly. This poses a challenge for educationalists who think only in terms of league tables and learning to be 'fit for purpose': which today means to be workhorses on the treadmill of economic advancement.

The timeless revolution will be as big and as speedy as the technological revolution. Communications on the inner planes will be even quicker than they are becoming on the outer planes. There will be communication in cyberspace without the need for computers. Yet the current obsession with communications technology is a perfect metaphor and training tool for extraordinary things to come.

Computers, for good or ill, are changing the nature of the brains of young people today. On the one hand they are creating a shortened attention span, and on the other they are training the synapses to join up more rapidly, enhancing the speed of the brain. Young people are keeping up to speed with their speedy synapse discoveries. Indeed, the brains of children will eventually have acquired the tools to communicate more and more easily with 'all that is'.

Children and young people will achieve quite naturally what it has taken eons for committed, older individuals to achieve through a lifetime of journeying to consciousness. And in that natural communication, the new children of integrity will simply *be*; open and alive to the richness and texture of what it is to exist in a new world of infinite loving kindness.

CONDUCT MORE BECOMING

There needs to be a new code of conduct established for all human beings; like the Ten Commandments, but not so judgemental. A '*Mercy Commandments*' list of all those qualities required in a thinking, feeling, demonstrative society, where all are equal and all are ready to put down their lives for the cause of universal harmony. By which we mean – in a living sense – committing thoroughly to the idea of a new world view. A commitment that encompasses all of who you are, not just demonstrated one day a week, or twice a year during religious festivities.

This list would ask all mankind to honour others in every way they can, in every situation they find themselves in. Coming to the conclusion that all people are equal is the hardest conclusion of all, and yet it is true. And in that truth you must operate your 'mindful' existence, because it is this truth that is the foundation of the new world view.

Becoming quieter will allow you to see that silence is indeed golden. The inner voice cannot be heard with so much noise and clatter around you. The gifts of techno-communications are far outweighed by the noise they bring. The clatter, the chatter and the noise of modern life are highly detrimental to listening on the inner planes of consciousness. Try it. Try being silent for an hour a day, a minute a day: to contemplate quietly the meaning of who you are and why you are here.

Taking time to speak wisely is such a pleasure now. By 'speaking wisely' you speak with greater awareness of what you are saying, to whom you are saying it and how you are gesturing what you are saying. Mindful of this, the world becomes more solidly based in truth; more gentle to be in. Gentle truth is so much more comfortable than harsh truth. Harsh truth is judge-mental and edgy; gentle truth is honouring and forceful.

Being small is so much nicer than needing to feel big. Remaining small in the confines of the grandeur of who you truly are is more truthful than the inflation you transmit when you fear you are not significant enough. The small of life is much more powerful than the inflation of life. Living in the small is more than big enough.

How different the world would be if all the politicians and bankers and insecure people who have needed to inflate themselves, were to live in the force of the small. How much fuller, more gentle and more effective they would be, and more useful to the rest of humanity.

Everything is becoming simpler, despite outwards appear-ances. It is simple to be small; it is simple to be silent, simple to become an ambassador for peace and understanding. It takes far less energy to be truthful and simple. When energy spent on the inner planes is less, so miraculously the energy consumed on the outer planes will be less: inner and outer, macro and micro. The world is a replica of the living, breathing universe.

How beautiful is this simplicity, this quietness, this inner smallness, when all around are chattering nineteen to the dozen, and the clattering is like a busy railway station.

'Nothing ventured, nothing gained' is the final 'Commandment' now. It is time to put it all to the test, to try it out. It is time to make the commitment to change and not just talk about it in hallowed terms.

It is 'Holy' to add this quiet dimension to our lives, but Holy in a material, visceral sense. This quietness and smallness and 'meekness' must be taken right inside the body, not just into the head or even just into the heart. The whole body is engaged in this change, from top to toe. How else can spirit enter the earth if not, like a lightning conductor, through the whole human body?

A BODY FIT FOR LIGHT

How do we open the whole body to Light? We open it through the 'centres' of our being: the chakra points of ancient Indian wisdom. And we open up these centres to spirit through the understanding that all parts of our body have input to meaning as well as a physical function, and they desire inner peace. The significance of these centres needs to be understood and included as part of the sum total of what it takes for man to become whole and spiritualised and useful to planetary living.

So it is not only the head or the heart that dictates a person's actions. In fact he or she will more often be 'centred' naturally in a completely different place in the body than they might have imagined. And it is through this centre that they will eventually access the most information about their true spiritual nature.

It is important to place your trust in the body and think its responses through to their logical conclusions. When one part of your body continually brings hurt and pain or is always the first to lack energy, this part is often asking to come into view. It is asking to express the meaning behind it: creatively, spiritually, motivationally. While the rest of your body acts as the *aide memoire*, it may be that the 'centre' connected to this part of your body has the greatest potential to express who you are.

You do not touch the stars by levitating: you touch them by listening deeply inside yourself to everything the body has to say. By listening deeply and luxuriating in the sound of silence within you, the bells start to ring, and the imagination opens up to the threshold of Life itself.

How can that be?

God made man in his own image. In other words, the essence of man is the essence of the universe. Only man came together in the exact image of multidimensional, universal understanding. Only man has the miraculous sum of the constituent parts of atoms and molecules, elements and enzymes, with the potential to mirror universal loving kindness.

So how else would man reach the stars, if not by examining everything he is made of; everything that is changing within him, physically, emotionally, mentally and spiritually? We are our own best libraries of congress, our own best litmus test for everything that is happening in universal law. How else could man reach the stars but through the auspices of his own loving kindness? It's as simple as that. 'Know Thyself' through and through.

NEW TIMES

Our time is nearly at an end. The Lords of Time have brought humanity to this point of timelessness; the multidimensional understanding that man is the mirror of the universe in time. Timelessness will prevail now within the human framework. Yes, a two-tier, simultaneous life of time and timelessness is possible now.

Those who can live this dual life will sail on the wings of timelessness. Those who cannot manage timelessness will continue to walk under the weight of time. Oh for the wings of a dove to wander far away into the inner realms of all that is. Timelessness will bring such rewards that humanity will never be the same again.

Our time is over. We, the Lords of Time, will retreat into universal timelessness for all time now. Our time is no longer needed. The Lords of Time will retreat for the next ten million years, allowing human beings to make their choices, make their mistakes, through the auspices of loving kindness.

Our time is no longer your time. We are unable to help you further. The akashic records will no longer be available. The recognition of rhythms and cycles, time and tides, will no longer apply in the same way as the moon moves away and out of orbit of the earth. The moon will no longer have jurisdiction over man's well-being.

It will no longer be possible to remember how you got here, how you lived through eons and eons of time to reach this place of integration and understanding. All the records will be lost to the inner gaze. Human beings will no longer know why they are here or why they came from God. You will simply know that you are here, living in a multidimensional universe and in touch with all that is.

What a promise; what a rebirth; what a privilege. What a responsibility, as the world turns to a different tune, a different note, and a different recognition of its central place in a dynamic universe. And as these things come into view, through the inner gaze, there will be a happiness of spirit, and greater under-standing of current dilemmas. There will be distinction and merit in being human, no longer carrying the underlying shame and blame that pervades humanity now.

Pie in the sky? Perhaps.

But already there are those who know this truth, and whose beauty is shining into the environment sufficiently for others to know that something is up. There is a sense in the air that the game is up: that there is a disturbance to complacency and to endless drama.

Dig deep into your soul now; bring out the best in yourself before it is too late. You can continue to live in the miasma of fantasy or bring yourself up to date and into the environment of truth; where real time is no time and everything takes on a different hue and a different speed. A new day is a new dawn, every day. In this chaotic world you live in fear. In the new world you can attain stability, rhythm and happiness. Man has come of age. Have you?

ALL WILL BE REVEALED

There has always been prophecy that '*All will be revealed*'; that '*The Kingdom will come*'. We are here as proof that Time will tell. Time will become the issue of the decade and time will appear to elongate not truncate. It will seem as though the clock suddenly stops, and all that rushing will seem silly. The lemmings may still rush over the cliff, but those who are able to stop, to live in timelessness, will feel themselves living in a new universe altogether.

The 'rushers' will look silly, the 'toffs' and 'chavs' will seem silly. All extremes of separation will look sillier and sillier, while the 'middle ground', the sensible citizens, will begin to hold their own. All will feel separate, and different and in league with life, along with the rest of humanity.

No more 'down tools' on operating as a normal human being; no need to make your mark on society by being irredeemably different to everyone else. There is safety and happiness in numbers, in community, in social interaction of a simple and thoughtful kind.

This is a different universe, a different understanding of what it is to be human; of what it is to be a useful member of society, without needing to stand out from the rest. All human beings will stand out from the rest through the intrinsic understanding of their own self-worth. They will be certain in their own needs and wants and secure in their sense of self-responsibility and social understanding.

Everyone will know they are valuable, interesting and

individual human beings, and seen by others for their uniqueness and the pleasurable environment they inhabit. Gentle harmony for all humanity is the key to Life Everlasting.

Is this possible? Of course it is.

The recipe for Life Everlasting is a real understanding that humanity was meant to be peaceable, alive in the image of God. Not the warring community it has been where winner takes all and devil takes the hindmost; the devil of self-contempt, self-abuse, self-negation. That is the devil you are fighting; nothing more than your own self-imposed devilment. Why give heed to the devil now? Turn him away and live your life to the fullest possible extent. Be the most creative, the most content, the most simple you can be.

Alas, for so many people at this time, 'simple' sounds dull and non-expressive. Making a mark takes courage and determination and then, for many, it means feeling superior and special.

Even now, as we speak, there is a period of enlightenment opening up in the universal need for peace. No matter how bad it looks, mankind is emerging in such beautiful proportion now. It cannot be long before the universal input of loving kindness reveals to man the less base nature of himself. It is easy to say, of course, when the world is shattering in front of our eyes, but no one has been left untouched by the recent demise of trust in the old ways of doing things.

Inside everyone a seed has now been sown. This is the seed of a humanity that all mankind has wished for: a race of beings that is good and understandable; a race imbued with the ethical aspects of decency and integrity. The intention itself has everything in its favour. The universal understanding of God's loving kindness is already beginning to take effect.

In that one moment of time when everyone on the planet wished mankind to be a better race, the intention was set in stone. When it crossed people's minds – even the most hardened control freaks – that mankind could not survive in this fashion of greed and non-sustainability, the world turned on its axis and a new era was begun. Humanity was on the right trajectory towards becoming a more equal, sustainable, loving anchor for universal change and harmony.

In the course of time, quietly, independently, and according to their unique potential, everyone will have the opportunity to make their mark, and fulfil their inalienable right to be a valued human being on planet earth.

And so be it.

PART TWO:
THE PRACTICAL GUIDE

"We are good primates so we spend most of our time maintaining and defending our territory, so that it will protect and gratify us; climbing – or trying not to slide down – the tribe's hierarchical ladder. We talk about love, about good and evil, philosophy and civilisation and we cling to these respectable icons the way a tick clings to its nice big warm dog."

Muriel Barbery: *The Elegance of the Hedgehog*

We look around us and see greed. We see the chaos that has ensued from the 'must have' and 'must have it now' ideology that has washed over us in the last twenty years or so. And we see now how the addictive, material nature of man is coming back to haunt us.

Astrology is a brilliant map. More than twenty-five years ago, Liz Greene, the psychological astrologer and writer, said that when Pluto moved into the sign of Sagittarius (in 1995) we would see the rise of religious fundamentalism of all kinds. Australian astrologer Ed Tamplin described this transit as a time when the IT revolution would gather pace, taking world communications to another level of satellite sophistication. When the time came they were both proved to be right.

Pluto takes roughly eighteen years to transit through each sign, and Ed Tamplin explains that Pluto's powerful effect is to act as a catalyst for worldly change, akin to "splitting the tiny atom and producing a massive nuclear explosion". Once again Pluto is ready to rock our world. It first moved into the corporate sign of Capricorn on January 25th 2008, and finally entered it properly in January 2009.

Says Ed Tamplin: "Capricorn governs the wheels that turn our society, its administration, pillars, traditions and institutions. Pluto refers to custom and convention, only to challenge and change it. The archetypal resonance of Pluto is one of cathartic and evolutionary transformation. Pluto's mythological associations with death and rebirth define the principle that breakdown and decay are an essential part of the ongoing life process."

There is nothing more resonant than this description of our current position. We watch the destablising of our fundamental institutions and the crumbling of our cherished structures. It brings fear that we are unsupported in any shape or form and out of control. Yet it is a chaos that has been waiting to happen, a time to come face to face with our folly in thinking we are only material beings.

ADDICTION TO CONTROL

It is systematic that 'power over others' dictates the old world view. Governments take every opportunity to tighten control, to make themselves the arbiters of how things need to be. There are systems in the world in which one person powers over all the others.

This isn't the way it should be. We need to see that controlling others is absolutely abhorrent. Indeed, *loss of control* might be seen as a way of life at this time. At the same time, more than ever, we must learn to become self-motivated, self-driven and self-sustained. This is not impossible.

GUIDELINES:

In the current situation more and more people are asking themselves questions; sitting down quietly and reflecting on the need to understand themselves more fully as human beings, without a God sitting in judgement. In fact, it is interesting to ponder that it is the old view of 'God sitting in judgement' that has inspired the human race to exhibit this God-like power over others.

The way forward at this perplexing time is to experience the planet as an interconnected system, and not as a hierarchical system with God in control. In the world as we know it, we all hold the paradox of what it is to be human. On the one hand we have a sense that we are 'special', and on the other hand that we are 'unworthy'. Until now we have lived in a paradoxical world of dominance and servility, and each person has had the opportunity either to become a God or to become a slave to God's Will or a mixture of both.

But it is time to perceive that there is no exterior figure that demands that we should become better human beings and punishes us if we do not. This does not mean there is no emotional tie to the Godhead. What it does mean is that our dominant personality and our slave personality are being given the opportunity to integrate. We can metamorphose into a kind of human being who has dominion over himself.

The old way will not work. Within the next few years we will get the real sense that dictators, controllers and politicians who do not understand the need to integrate these profound opposites in order to experience a fairer world, will no longer feel themselves to be powerful. When a man or a woman no longer feels powerful, then they no longer command the respect and honouring to be chosen as a leader.

For example, at the time of his election in 2008, the leadership that President Obama offered was regarded with respect. He has a natural energy of integration that emanates from his being and in that moment it called people towards him. There is within Mr Obama no sense of 'powering over'. That is fact. And when other leaders see this inspirational figure commanding respect, they become insecure in their own need to pursue dominion over others.

When people are greedy they wish to have power, and once they have power they wish to have power over others. And where you have power over others, there will always be those who play out the opposite and feel they are victims and slaves.

We see the madness of power bringing more and more chaos, as we do with despotic dictators throughout the world - and often much closer to home. We have seen Fundamentalists of all religions fighting for their lives. The incidence of bullying in schools is unprecedented, including sexual bullying. There is unbridled fear of loss of control and power: witnessed in the hysteria of electioneering worldwide.

We have seen that since the beginning of time man has lived with the duality of Spirit (of God's dominion over) and Matter, which like a machine allows people to do instinctively what they are programmed to do. It is the 'selfish gene' idea that human beings are cogs in the wheel of a machine that simply promulgates power and survival of the fittest. In playing out of this duality there are those who see themselves as God and those who remain slaves to matter.

But now, in this extraordinary moment in time, the balances of power are changing, when the old control and dominion over others simply cannot maintain its structure. Life really is shifting away from this unworkable, emotionally-charged duality of slave and master, victor and victim.

The realignment to *independence and interdependence* through loving kindness is now the way forward, not control by one person over another through power and influence. Loving kindness is a clear, pure, detached experience, not the emotionally-charged sense of conditional love we often use in our fight for control.

There is now an opportunity for the most extraordinary change of emphasis of what it is to be human; as big a leap as the fish evolving from the sea to the amphibian, to the ape, to the human being as we know it now. Still carrying the vestiges of our history, humanity will begin to experience itself as a different race, integrating greater universal energies of spiritual awareness based on loving kindness.

BLOGGING OUR LIFE AWAY: THE INFORMATION AGE

There is a tyranny to social networking! Like, socially you're dead if you don't have hundreds of 'friends' out there. That seems to be true for younger people anyway. Offering opportunities for everyone to have a view, each as valid as the next is good. But sharing every jot and nuance of personal thoughts and feelings that used to be private – shared only with a diary and your best friend – is daunting. Broadcasting into cyberspace for everyone to see and, what is worse, to comment on, is demanding.

There is so much chat! What happened to silence and, most important, to reflection?

GUIDELINES:

Thinking of cyberspace allows us to reflect on the fact that we are all part of a vast and vibrant universal energy system. Imagine breaking down this vast broadband system into layers and layers of information, and then believe that this is an experience every human being can take part in, without the intermediary of a computer!

It is time to open up in consciousness to the real meaning and enormity of the *Information Age*. And by information age we mean the totality of the experience of cyberspace.

The cyberspace of the Internet is in fact a very material one. It is within the realms of matter that broadband exists. It is as though broadband is circulating through the material dimension of human experience. Which is why pornography and consumerism run rife on the Internet.

In the old order the material plane is the instinctive plane. It is a closed system. It cannot link into the higher realms of information in cyberspace and never will. However much the technologists believe the machine can ultimately be king, it can never match the human being, which is the only instrument that can meet the other dimensions in cyberspace.

In many ways this is already causing disturbances in the energy fields in material dimensions of cyberspace – witnessed in the chaotic times we live in. Giving away your secrets to other people means that you are inviting other people to feed on your energy. You become less and less boundaried by who you are and who you could become.

To earn the right to become spiritualised and thus able to enter the deeper, meaningful realms of inner cyberspace, you have to refine and define yourself more and more and more. But while you allow yourself to be 'eaten' by other people – who are often so 'hungry' through their own deficiencies and woundedness – you become less and less able to maintain the shape of who you are.

The addictive arenas of pornography and unbridled consumerism are the outcome of a feeding frenzy by people who are unable to maintain their own individuality. It is as though they are voraciously feeding from the troughs of energy that meet their lower needs.

The Internet itself is harmless. It is a neutral force, the outer, material experience of what is happening universally. It is the symbol on the lower planes of the increasing availability of information, and part of the great evolution of communication between the earth and the universe. It is those who become attuned to its wisdom, through understanding that they are spiritualised beings in a material body, who will access more and more of 'all that is' in cyberspace.

Created in its own image, the Godhead wants every human being to experience the universal principle of detached loving kindness. The Godhead is a congruence of inclusiveness; it is the energy that holds the universe in balance, in stasis, to the extent that everything is revolving around something else and maintains its integrity, until it is ready to move on. But in that moving on, it does not disturb the order, the cohesion and the meaning of the universe that we inhabit at this time.

The Godhead is the thought behind the whole of cyberspace that it is possible to experience in this universe. There are many who have attained sufficient stringency in their 'growing up' to know themselves truly as spiritualised beings with a task to fulfil – which is to move and have their being in the myriad layers of cyberspace.

In many ways, it is the lack of discipline and lack of boundaries today that prevent young people from becoming 'ensouled' and therefore unable to reach cyberspace other than in the material plane. In years to come blogging, for example, will lose its glamour and slow down, because opening up the airwaves in this way is actually exposing your soul for other peoples' consumption. The boundaries of the soul are flimsy, and can be 'eaten up' by other people. The more sensitive you are, the more you might feel 'consumed' even now.

Yet the Internet itself is a living correspondence and metaphor for our ability to own and express our true magnificence. In fact the Internet is actually changing peoples' brains – as some neuroscientists fear. But in doing so it is paradoxically creating the ability to think laterally and to shift gears with sufficient rapidity to link to the multidimensional universe. It is doing so in a way that nothing else has been able to achieve until now.

In other words, young people can, with imagination and understanding, equip themselves with the exact mind strength to penetrate and move and have their being in the 'Divine' aspects of cyberspace. It is the addiction to the material and to the destruction rather than the building of relationships that prevents it.

The dilemmas of young people today are as great as, but different from, those of previous generations. Yet all generational dilemmas offer the challenges needed for us to become aware of spiritualised humanity, and enable us to access more and more of the truth, beauty and loving kindness of the universe we live in.

GROWING OUR OWN VALUE SYSTEM

Energy follows thought. Beware what you think and dream. If you grab an inspiration or an idea or a 'certainty', the universe colludes to reinforce that idea. You will hear a chance interview; have a conversation; pick up a book or a newspaper, and find, somehow, it echoes what you were thinking and feeling. Little by little you grow your own picture, for better or worse, positive or negative, pessimistic or optimistic. In other words, we can and do create our own world view.

The magic still works. The universe colludes to grow our own picture. But how carefully we have to look at everything we experience, and endeavour to start with clarity and truth. Others are magnetised by our truth and we by that of others. For good or ill, we bring into our environment those people who resonate with our own picture, and corroborate our 'truth'. Our energy will magnetise others of like mind and attitude.

How important it is to know, as certainly as we can, that we are clear of prejudices and unconscious mechanisms, and confident of perceiving our truth with integrity – especially if we want to share it with others.

Remember that what we do is sure to come back to us. It is a law of the universe. If you behave badly, life will behave badly to you. If you hurt someone, somewhere along the line you are hurt in exactly the same measure. Conversely, if we think positively we create a wave of positivism. Being helpful creates a wave of helpfulness. Thinking beauty allows beauty to surround us. By being happy we allow happiness to ripple out into the wider environment.

How clever it all is. And when you trust in that cleverness, you can grow your own world view and nourish your own truth from whichever point you pick it up. Like the discovery in mathematics of the infinite beauty and expanding nature of the fractal in the Mandelbrot Set, creativity can start anywhere and grow organically, defying chaos, into infinity. This way of growing is organic and not directed or decided; it unfolds, as though truth is spun and woven within itself.

GUIDELINES:
The best way to create a world that is honest, fair and without prejudice is to make the effort to stay integrated; not to let old hurts and slights pop up through the cracks from the uncon-scious. Unless you are vigilant old wounds and old ideologies will surface and allow in those negative fears and responses that catch you unawares.

Making *value judgements*, however, is not necessarily a bad thing. Discrimination is always important. In every decision, every reflection and every allowance made, there might always be someone else's unconscious projections and intentions to be taken into the equation.

Nonetheless it is important to be aware just how pernicious are the unconscious frailties that create our own judgements, and which come from difficulties or prejudices absorbed in childhood, or attitudes instilled from other sources.

Releasing the unconscious of its debilitating personal and collective history is now absolutely vital. It is the only way to proceed, if we wish to maintain the sharpest intuition about the world around us and become the clearest channels for spiritualised values on planet earth. Unless we do so, even what appear to be the most considered and rational positions will, in fact, come from unconscious reactions to our woundedness. Most of us operate from the safety of habit, too fearful to change.

Whether we admit it or not, most people feel unsafe in the milieu of being human. Everything we do is shaped to shore up our safety: whether it is a learned response to any given situation or a ritualised way of behaving out in the world. Most people choose their path in life according to the tune of the unconscious demands they are dancing to.

When we can listen and respond to those unconscious demands in an enlightened way, we can begin to look with confidence at why we are who we are, and why we do what we do. We can begin to unburden ourselves and release the incredible pressures we put on ourselves to do what, more often than not, we should not be doing.

By discovering that we respond in an automated, reactive fashion according to our unconscious processes, the first step is to reflect on our everyday behaviour and ask 'why did I do that'? 'What made me think that?' 'I don't like my response to that'. In this way we begin to recognise that the drive to think and feel and control many things in our lives comes from a 'demand' that feels inevitable. We need to think where it comes from or why a behaviour comes in that particular form.

Despite the lack of scientific proof of its effectiveness, the UK government is now spending huge amounts of money on Cognitive Behavioural Therapy units. There is now some recognition that destructive thoughts and behaviours can rule our lives unnecessarily and that 'talking therapies' can be life changing.

Many more people are now acknowledging the chaos they feel inside themselves and that their lives are making less and less sense. This confusion is corroborated when they see things happening in the outside world: like the nonsensical edicts of 'political correctness' or the stubborn responses of the 'jobsworth' mentality. It is as though unconscious processes and prejudices are running rife in the world.

It appears that there is no longer the control or discipline within individuals to start the process of taking stock. We do not check the responses we make when we feel out of control or misunderstood. We know this isn't the kind of behaviour we would wish for ourselves, yet we cannot quite say, "Stop, this is enough."

It is time to reflect. We must reposition what is valuable, remember what is significant and intuit what is most important for us, and every individual on the planet. We can no longer support rampant greed or a rampant need for power, or condone that people live like automatons, or ignore those who deliberately 'up the anti' in order to create even more chaos at a time of incredible global stress.

Fortunately there are many who have long experienced themselves as 'not really themselves' in a consumerist world that has become even more material and addictive, and where values and integrity are virtually non-existent.

This is a moment for a collective 'stopping'. Paradoxically and symbolically, the recent halt of the global money flow has been an opportunity to facilitate that end and to prevent the world from going mad. Money, power and greed as the motivating value system for the planet, brings the earth to its densest materiality. There is either potential collapse or a renewed spiritual understanding that the meaning of existence bears no relationship to money or to greed or possessions per se.

What matters is the bigger picture, the relationship to a Godhead that wishes to experience loving kindness as its motivating force. What is important is that people understand who they are in the world and the universe they live in. To realise themselves in wisdom, beauty and truth, and to know they have the ability to create a world in their own mind's eye that is full, rich, and all consuming. And, as the picture grows, for each individual to see how the image of their outer life can change, in the most extraordinary and magical ways.

It is not difficult. There are many young people who are now struggling with the grossness and the density of the material world. Like the autistic children rendered speechless by the density of the 'brick wall' they feel inside themselves, who are sensitive to a different world view. It is a world view that often consists of equations that describe the meaning of a vast and beautiful universe, not the grubby, limiting density of materiality, full of greed and illusion.

Empires and ideologies reach base level before they collapse. Everything happening at this time is in transition in preparation for the 'Phoenix to rise'. We can surely begin to change our picture of what it is to be human on planet earth, and part of every other dimension of the universal environment.

There is so much more creative imagination within each human than you could ever imagine. Anything that crosses your mind, any fleeting picture of something wise, something different, something amazing, can be noted and added to a burgeoning picture of the new and beautiful. Silence helps you respond to these small stimuli and enables them to penetrate the current dense reality. Just let them in and let them grow.

LEARNING IS THE MEANING OF LIFE

In the film *To Sir with Love* the teacher, played by Sidney Poitier, called his pupils by name, individualised them all and made them feel important. Gradually there was a sense that everyone fitted into the class, was respected and treated with politeness.

Politeness is such a different approach to the new demand for Respect. Politeness feels very still and almost passive, while respect, in the way it has been adopted today, feels impolite, demanding and sometimes scarily aggressive. Politeness has a different weight, a different elegance. In such awareness there is no bolstering of position by suppressing or bullying someone weaker.

Sooner or later the most extraordinary changes will occur in the minds of men and woman who will know that education must change not only for the technological revolution but also for a new value system.

When you are polite, respect comes naturally. Politeness is a self-contained way of being, and makes no demands on anyone else. To be polite is to be detached. It contains the element of individuality that those who aggressively demand respect do not have in their herd mentality. It is the herd mentality that demands to be different and individual.

GUIDELINES:

If politeness were the *lingua franca* taught to children in school, rather than respect, it would bring a new kind of community. Individuality and detachment would lead not to a herd, but to a *community* of individual children. The bullying would have to cease.

In a herd there is always the top dog in any situation. With politeness and individuality you just get on with being who and what you are without controlling anyone else. It is simple: the child who is polite is more individual than the child who demands respect and claims to be different.

Children can become individuals from the age of three if they are taught politeness: in school, in kindergarten, in reception, in nursery. Politeness is the key to a new beginning for a new humanity that is detached, individual and community minded.

If a class of five-year-olds stands up when the teacher comes into the room and individually say 'good morning Miss Brown', and Miss Brown acknowledges each child individually, the feeling inside each child as well as the teacher is a natural respect.

When the children feel individual and appreciated, and not treated by the teacher as a herd, they will reciprocate. They will greet each other in a warm feeling of community, with a charm and respect for each other. There can be relief all round as the primal aspect of the herd gives way to a sense of the individual in the community and at home.

This is a different picture, a different world, centred in a different place in the physical body. It creates a new equilibrium in the body itself, centred in the cooler solar plexus of individuality, rather than in the sacral centre of the herd, which encourages rampancy and greed, or in the over excitable and emotional centre of the heart.

The new child, who lives more comfortably in his own skin, has the community at heart. He has a sensible approach to resources and the environment and does not feel greedy. It is a change from the primal, instinctual to the thoughtful and rational at this time. By the age of five he can begin to know for himself what he needs and it is not a huge amount. One pencil, one crayon, or simply access to a pool of crayons.

Education has come to a standstill in some ways. It is at an end point. There is no further place to go and it is time for a u-turn. It is time to recognise that education is not about grades and targets, but about the nurturing of individual talents and predispositions and the extraordinarily unique qualities that children are bringing into incarnation right now.

There can no longer be a one-child policy, a one-direction policy at a time when everything is changing so radically. The education system is minimising the experience of the child, not maximising the experience of unique individuals.

Everyone can see that children are different now. These are the souls who have come to take us by the hand; to open us up to the earth's explosive introduction into universal understanding.

These new children cannot withstand the directive, competitive energies that mark education as it stands now. When they are 'hoodwinked' into the strait jacket that competitive education demands, they are far too sensitive. They shriek that it does not work for them.

Young children shriek when everything around them is too controlled, too tight and too demanding; when they are forced to fit into parental expectations – or parental indifference.

Every child that shrieks seems to be demanding that they are seen as new children, different children, experiencing life in a completely different way to their older siblings and to the way parental demands expect.

We need to look hard at what these children are saying when they ask to be left alone. We need to see why they demand to take a break from the energetic demands of the rest of the class which expects them to drop everything they are experiencing to become what other people want of them; which is to become one of them.

Spiritual Scientist, Rudolf Steiner, was correct when he indicated that until the age of seven a child is not ready to think numbers. But when the child is seven, when numbers are experienced as the energetic resonance through which the world moves and has its being, he can experience the joy that numbers bring.

That is a constant. Children for whom numbers are an intrinsic experience become demented and disenchanted when taught to add and subtract in a linear fashion. In fact, they have the most enjoyable, uninhibited way of becoming educated by themselves. When teaching begins with the experience of numbers, rather than awarding marks for adding and subtracting in a linear fashion, there will be a very extraordinary shift in the moral compass of children.

Making children do formal dance is unproductive at this time. Formal dance does not allow the child to 'become the orchestra that makes him dance'. Instead he is simply the instrument of the structured movement. For Swiss musician Jacques Dalcroze, who devised Eurhythmics, the idea of music and free movement was far more creative. And so it should be for these newly different children who are directed, unsuitably, to ballet or tap or ballroom classes.

These children need to be the orchestra, to dance freely and joyfully, as though they are all the instruments. When they are seen as unique beings in the new universal environment of our time, it is as though universal harmony, universal number, universal enjoyment is now able to flow through these children without hindrance.

Education needs to become more 'people centred'. By which we mean not child centred and selfishness centred, but other people centred. As though there is in the world another person who is more important than me. In people centred education there can exist a race of young people who have a sense of working in the world of men and women as a contributor rather than a taker.

The education of our youngsters needs to be tailored to the idea that each child is now a child of the universe, a child of many different skills, dimensional experiences and understandings. Each child needs to be nurtured within an environment in which all children are individually nurtured for their experiences, skills and understandings, but where none is better than the other, and no one is competing against another. Each becomes one amongst a number of special, unique and extraordinary human beings in a world of loving kindness.

TAKING YOURSELF SERIOUSLY

It is part of the negative and positive aspect of current humanity's dualistic nature that we either 'stand too far forward' and believe ourselves to be inordinately 'special', or to stand too far back and experience ourselves as insecure and unworthy. It is in the integration of opposites at this time that we can begin to see ourselves as extraordinary in our ordinariness, and, most important, to take seriously the issue of self-worth.

GUIDELINES:

Self-worth is in fact the hardest thing for humans to really understand at this time. People have become so muddled in their view of their own self-worth – a view that is actually totally inaccurate – that sometimes they do not even know they are lacking confidence in who and what they are.

This overlay of confidence has much to do with the greed, the grasping, or the yearning for 'fifteen minutes of fame'. But underneath it all is a lack of self-worth, which until now has been 'in the genes' of what it is to be human.

It is intrinsically difficult for human beings to believe that they are worthy of other people's regard. They are insecure in knowing themselves to be wholly okay in the process of becoming valued human beings on planet earth. They cannot trust that they have a valued task, and the opportunity to become their full, creative potential, and wise personalities imbued with soul consciousness.

So we are unaware that all our aspirations and ambitions stem from the feeling that we are not enough in the way we exist already. We need to recognise that the most important aspect of becoming a new human being is to see that it is self-worth that is the main target, the main experience that will really change our sense of ourselves in human form.

When people are striving for celebrity or money or to be better than they really are, it is lack of self-worth that is driving the engine. It is as if the drive to value ourselves via money or celebrity or fame is a surrogate for opening up to our value as a human being. It is time to be recognised for the vastness of our spirit and soul. Not to be defined by what other people think of us, and how much we have achieved through the insecurities of our ambition and drive.

It is our purpose now to value ourselves; to recognise that in the now moment we have all we need to become all that we are, and to realise that this does not require acquiring more and more and more. It means that in the wee small hours we can meditate on our sense of self-worth, and that this can happen quite naturally and easily.

In this simple meditation of self-worth, allow yourself to imagine and experience a Being in front of you. This being has within it all the makings of one who feels beautiful, richly encompassed by love and comfort. In forgetting Self, allow in a real exposure to the stature and wondrous vitality of this being, who can become a mentor, a real experience within your senses.

Allow this to be a visceral experience of what it feels like to be full of worth, full of self-worth, full of interesting ideals that become intriguing to the senses. Allow yourself to know how it feels to be this person, this example that has come to you in the small hours when you feel you have 'blown it', or you have not met expectations – whether of your peers or your boss or your siblings – and you feel wretched.

It is as though each time you allow this being to enter your space, your environment, it becomes more familiar to you. Simply by coming face to face with a being who you feel within your heart holds what it is to be worthy and everything you could wish to be, this familiarity becomes more and more automatic and acceptable and recognisable.

And each time you feel this being in your inner space, you come to know that it is truly connected to you, and in due time it is somehow in your best interests to recognise and accept that you and it are one. One morning or one evening there isn't any doubt. This friend, this being, this familiar alter ego, is very clearly who you are and who you wish to be. It holds everything you need to know about yourself as a worthy human being.

It is a visceral feeling, an embodied feeling. It is important that you and everything you are, is embodied in the here and now. It is as though, in this moment, you have stepped into a real understanding of what it is to have self-worth on planet earth, and not feel up against all the other human beings who make you feel insecure or inadequate, or rejected in this world.

Some people who feel of little worth have a tendency to hide; to sit alone; perhaps to make friends through cyberspace and the virtual world. It is easier to stay hidden and continue to protect yourself from those unworthy feelings in the world of men and women.

For others it means partying, binge drinking and having sex, just to stay in the loop of feeling of worth. Both behaviours bring you back to yourself in a self-negating, self-loathing and, at times, self-harming way.

It is time to allow in our spiritual being, our real friend, our real sense of self-worth. In these chaotic times, those who hide from humanity and those who hit it full on are yearning to find themselves in a different way.

Give it a go. Experience it as an exercise, as a game, as a delight, as an understanding that there is more to who you are than your failed sense of 'keeping up with the Joneses', or having a million 'friends' on Facebook. It is time to 'know thyself' in any way possible. It is time to acknowledge that your Self is longing to know you.

When you feel there is someone who longs to know you, who longs to be your friend, who longs to give you everything you could ever wish for, how cool is that? How satisfying is that?

It is not as though either your attempts at venturing out into the world, blagging your way through, or hiding in here, hiding behind the screen, have given you any more worth than you had before.

Give it a try. Give it an understanding that the inner friend, the inner experience is where the sense of worth comes. No exterior accolades, no exterior fan club will ever change how you feel about yourself. Only you can do that. Only you can take responsibility for yourself in this way. Allow this real sense of Self to enter your life right now.

MONEY IS THE ROOT OF ALL CHANGE

As Barack Obama says in *Audacity of Hope*, "Globalisation has greatly increased economic instability for millions of ordinary people. The result has been the emergence of what some call a 'winner-take-all' economy in which a rising tide doesn't necessarily lift all boats."

When we learn that an investment bank advises an entire country to 'gamble' with its assets to maximise profits, and is then seen to be betting on the certainty of it going bankrupt, we all lose heart. When we hear that debt companies buy the debt of a country for a knock down price, in order to cash in by charging high rates of interest when the country moves into credit, how much lower can we go? When politicians milk their countries' assets and steal from their own people, there seems very little hope.

GUIDELINES:

Money has become a commodity that is more important than anything that the money can buy. It is as though money itself has become the means by which everyone is valued. The more money they have, the more they are valued as a human being. It is as though money has become the object of worship rather than God Himself.

Money is the god of modern day existence. The things that money can buy are exploited because they cost money, not because they have a truth or a beauty or an aesthetic intrinsically indentured within them. They are merely an example of money.

Money is a commodity that becomes the thing to worship whenever there is a lack of faith and hope and charity within a culture. It is as though money becomes the God of Salvation, in place of the God in the heavens.

Yet, in the now moment there will be a real falling away of the idolatry of money. Already the bankers look like thieves and the people who are greedy are working themselves to death for the god of money; blowing themselves out younger and younger. When the god of money becomes God, then everything begins to tumble because humanity cannot sustain a life where God is now so physically imbued with what should be a spiritual experience.

Very often the gaining of money is a sexual urge, a primal urge, something to be 'thrust at' rather than earned for a job well done, to pay for things that have intrinsic worth to the one who buys it. In a very short time the god of money will simply have fallen like all idols fall. It is as flimsy as the paper it is written on.

In many ways the globalisation of everything at this time has held up to ridicule this sense of the winners and the losers and this idolatry of the god of money. And it is not coincidence that trust in God is less diminished in the 'have-nots' than in those with money. Those who crave riches have often lost faith in everything except the physical, the visceral, the sexual: the pornography of exploitation that the thrust for money has brought.

Money has become a dirty undertaking. It has become a corrupt undertaking. It has corrupted those who have dedicated their whole being to the acquisition of money. Those countries that have accepted money, that have co-opted to be the keepers of the money, have actually become more and more barren in terms of energetic resonance; in terms of the 'spirit of place' those countries now represent on planet earth.

There is a sterility about these countries that make money

their *raison d'être*. And when money is held acquisitively, secretively, there is distastefulness; a 'muckiness', a dark underbelly about the energy of that country.

Money is not evil. It is not the root of all evil. But in the present moment money is the machinery through which the shift will come. The growing recognition of the sterility of money will bring a reassessment of the notion that money is to be acquired for its own sake.

People will find meaning in the idea that money is firstly for buying what is needed to survive, and then for really appreciating the aesthetic, the meaning, the beauty and the substance of what that money has bought.

Remember that 'leisure' is the way to find meaning inside, not being overloaded with the busyness of modern life. It is time to think 'small', think 'enough', think 'meaning' – day by day by day. By doing so there will be a re-alignment of the relationship to money.

And when there is a renewed sense of the spirituality of what it is to be human, the idolatrous worship of money will disappear. It will give way to the unique, Divine and wonderful inner understanding that God is within, and to be worshipped as such. Then each individual will become aware that their sense of self-worth, and their consequent new responsibilities and understandings, will outweigh every other impulse – including the need to acquire money and make it a god.

When God is once again brought into the spiritual sphere of human understanding, there can no longer be yearning for money in the old way. Many people will change direction, change their viewpoint, and release their yearning urgency to have money.

There is something extremely beautiful about worship of the God-self within. The intense pleasure of knowing you are a bigger person, a magical person, a person of great wealth and wisdom, without being ruled by the wish for more and more money – certainly more than you need.

Those who wish to work in a caring capacity often feel unable to manage on the money they earn in the caring professions. It is time to recognise that caring will eventually become what everyone does naturally for everyone else. Caring is what happens in community. Care in the community will become the norm in a world full of loving kindness.

And people will begin to accept that money needs to be re-aligned in a very humane way. Those who have jobs that concern the welfare of others will be paid much more. While those who are working in the more exciting and glamorous jobs will know they must be paid much less.

This needs to be evolutionary change, evolutionary recognition that stems from the inner experience of true value and meaning, in a new world view in the process of becoming.

FACING THE TRUTH

There's a madness in the air. We can all feel it. We know the Emperor has no clothes, yet we collude in letting the madness continue.

We talk a lot these days about people who are 'in denial'. Politicians, for example, who blithely swear that black is white and never apologise for getting things wrong. Cheating sportsmen who deny wrongdoing when the evidence clearly proves otherwise. Journalists who break the law by hacking into private mobile phone conversations and insist their activities are in the public interest. We hear it, chat about it, shrug our shoulders and move on.

But what about you and me? Don't we, too, live in a miasma of self-denial? There is so much fantasy in the way we live today. We live beyond our means, yet feel we have a right to a certain way of life. Advertising – that elegant art of illusion – says so. We may live with a lurking sense of dread about it all, but fear to open our personal 'can of worms'. We keep a lid on things and continue to live instead in a world of virtual reality, like a long-running soap opera.

Self-delusion is a way of keeping safe, and keeping our confusion and anxiety at bay.

GUIDELINES:
The time has come for everyone to tell the truth as they see it. The trouble is that most people at this time actually see their own truth in a distorted light. Many people are under the influence of the Starship Enterprise! In other words there is a fantasy about living in the human body at this time that is carrying people away from truth like a Starship entering into another world altogether.

There is so little truth in most people's eyes that a miasma of delusion is now covering planet earth, in such a way that we see earth as a distortion of truth in every aspect of our understanding. A miasma of misunderstanding is covering earth and causing it to rock about like a ship in a storm or a plane in turbulence. It is making you sick and dizzy this Starship Enterprise!

What we ask you to do right now is to stop and think. Stop and feel. Stop and understand that the ship is actually quite out of control in some ways. And in many ways it is totally up to each individual to think about themselves in a new way, to think about their responses to their own actions, and trust that if they are willing to do this they will come out into the clearing of clear calm water.

We guarantee that the ship doesn't feel very calm at this time. There is so much anxiety and so much disconnection with the truth that people are beginning to feel like ships out of water. And we mix our metaphors because this is exactly what people on earth are doing at this time, mixing their metaphors: the scientific metaphor, the health metaphor, the eating metaphor, the drinking metaphor, the sleeping metaphor. All the metaphors are getting mixed and matched to such an extent that the way of life on planet earth is jumbled and unreal and untruthful. No one knows whether they are coming or going any more.

Is it really that bad? Well, yes and no. It is a bad moment in human history, this jumbling of the truth. You can feel the untruthfulness of life in the way everyone fails to tell the truth in every aspect of their lives: how they think, how they feel, how they resist things, attempt things, relate to things. Muddle is in the air because there is no truth to anything any more.

And yet, this is a golden moment, a golden opportunity for change and decision and making the effort to stay in your own truth; to face the truth within the heart of your being. It is an opportunity to become a citizen of earth in a more truthful and relevant way. An opportunity to bring into being the comfort and calmness you crave, but deny all the time by exciting the genes to change in ways that evolution does not deem responsible or desirable. In other words, this distortion of truth allows the mutation of the gene pool to lie to you, and create a monster of everything you ever felt yourself to be.

But you are not a monster. You are not bad; you are not a difficult person or a tyrant or a reckless being who needs to be punished. You need to be brave; you need to be constantly on the alert. But, above all, you need now the courage to open Pandora's Box. Allow the truth, in all its guises and all its monstrosities, to become clear to the conscious mind – before it devours you with distortions and disguises and recriminations.

We are here to guide you now in this truly magnificent enterprise. The Starship Enterprise is entering a new world view where truth, not fantasy, has the upper hand. It is the ride of a lifetime, this journey of opening up to truth.

In the current moment there is a storm in the heavens that needs to be understood, before the patina of truth can override the fantasy that has built up in the ethers of mankind. There is a Truth that has been waiting to descend on to planet earth since time immemorial. Until now, human beings have been treading the boards of an unfolding drama, in order to reach this point where a truthful relationship to the universe becomes possible.

In order to raise ourselves to this new level of truth and beauty, each of us must first release the sum total of tension that has accumulated within every human being since time began. The level of tension has now reached such proportions that earth has become like a huge organism waiting to explode. Yet it is through this explosion that humanity can move and have its being in the new truth.

However, we do not need to experience this explosion as a catastrophic event. It is possible for each individual to release the tension in his or her own being – by acknowledging and experiencing an outpouring of all the grief and sadness and misunderstanding that the world has accumulated since forever.

Within every individual is a deep sense of this sadness and grief that has accumulated throughout this life, and myriad former lifetimes. This now needs to be recognised, understood and let go.

To say that every human being is in-filled with grief and sadness may sound far-fetched but let us show you what we mean.

In your imagination, take a large ball and put it in your solar plexus. Allow this ball to feel so heavy that it begins to weigh you down – and down, and down and down. You begin to feel as though you have the weight of the whole world on your shoulders, yet are feeling it in your solar plexus.

Allow the ball to begin to open up, as though this weight has demons and unpleasant creatures tumbling out of it – just like the hell of those people in a Hieronymus Bosch painting. There is a deep sense of grief at their plight, their unseeing eyes, their fear and dissatisfaction.

Sense them descending into the earth with such rage and disappointment that you begin to feel the sadness of the earth receiving such creatures, when really it wants to feel joyous and happy and light-hearted. How can earth feel light-hearted with all this pain and grief opening up in its bowels?

This is how planet earth has felt since time immemorial, receiving the pain and sadness of humanity time after time after time: no wonder the earth did not want us. Oh no, the earth did not want this pain and sadness.

What we ask you to do now, however, is to close that gaping hole in the solar plexus. In your imagination allow it to heal with balm, and a beautiful, colourful cloth to bind it up. Feel the woundedness heal and disappear.

Now, open your heart to a deep sense of relief, and sigh and sigh and sigh. Know that you have closed that chapter on earth, and are now opening up the heart to the richness of being in love; in love with the world. Your heart is full of gratitude that all the tension, all that 'stickiness' has now disappeared from the planet. The heart is singing for joy and your whole being feels lighter and happier and released in a way you have never felt before.

Now come back to your solar plexus. Feel its emptiness, its pleasure at being free at last. Take a little bear, and put it in the solar plexus; a baby bear who is playing with Truth. What is truth? Truth is seeing yourself as a child who can play; a child who has options; a child who is teaching itself that life is good and happy and kind.

LIVING LIGHTLY

There is so much pressure to want more, not less. But we do know intuitively that we really are at danger point. As Oscar Wilde said 'we know everything and understand nothing'. Perhaps it is time to override what we think we want and look more carefully at what we truly need for a personally fulfilling life. Perhaps its time to downsize – in all appropriate ways – and discover that by doing so we can be more content than we ever believed possible. Desire for more is one of the most insidious aspects of our world today. If humanity desired wisdom a little more and 'stuff' a little less, we would realise that yearning for more is not the way to happiness – ever.

GUIDELINES:

No one who manifests greed will ever be able to manifest truth, beauty and wisdom. Perhaps that is a sweeping statement, but greed really is the antithesis of how human beings were meant to live in the world. The task of humanity has been to learn and then to understand what it means to be human to the fullest extent possible. Greed and a constant grasping for more reduces our ability to be still, to be silent, to 'wait on God' and feel ourselves to be participants and co-creators in the world of which we are a part. It is as simple as that.

Need versus greed is the secret metaphor for the right and wrong way to establish a new value system. And by getting the measure of our own well-being we can discover what our true needs are. Indeed, we can know that these needs can all be met – despite what we think is evidence to the contrary when we have set our sights so much higher.

Try this exercise.

Take a pen and make two columns on a sheet of paper. In the first column write a list of everything you feel you absolutely cannot do without in your life. List the things that you really think make you happy to have or do.

Then, in your mind's eye, hold each of these items for a good long moment in your solar plexus. *Feel carefully* what that item is saying. What does the most important 'must have' feel like now if you were to have less of it each week? Perhaps two glasses of wine each day instead of four are sufficient? Or if you were to eliminate it altogether? Perhaps swimming at the local leisure centre feels just as good as an expensive membership to the gym? Or a small car feels just as good as a flashy car – or suits you even better.

So now cross off the things you could completely do without.

Keep testing your items in the solar plexus. Become aware of what each thing means to you by concentrating hard and allowing the body to show you the truth. You will be surprised what the body knows compared to what your mind thinks it knows about these things.

Some of the items may make you sad to be without and of course you must retain them on your list. Reducing greed is not about making yourself miserable. But some apparent 'must haves' could actually make you feel unexpectedly nauseous or uneasy in some way and you'll be relieved to let them go in the most immediate way.

Put your current home in your solar plexus, and determine the truth about the way you need to live. It is actually possible that while one person might *need* a twelve-acre stately home, another would be perfectly happy in a beautifully styled bed-sit. We can honour ourselves in our disparate choices.

Look deeply and honestly at all the items on your list and feel the effect they have on your life for good or ill. Now write in the second column the complete but much reduced list you are left with, of the things you now know you need for a contented life. No one ever needs as much as they think they do. No one.

Relax in a chair and allow the new list in front of you to offer a new scenario, a new attitude to your life right now. Feel once again into the things you have chosen to make your life complete. Feel a sense of lightness inside as you contemplate what is important to you and why. How do you feel? Relieved? Frightened, because there is so little in life that you really need? Amazed?

Of course it takes great courage to make such changes in our lives. But, in the way of things, we cannot become aware of having more until there is a true understanding of wanting less.

Eventually there will be more and more people who will benefit enormously from a downsizing of needs and feel truly at peace with their smaller lifestyles. They will be the pioneers of a shift in consciousness that enables them to operate out of an innate creativity, through the dynamic of 'plasticity'.

Needs-based plasticity is simply the art of drawing to us everything we need to become totally self-sufficient and interestingly placed in the world. We cannot sustain a world where some people make money hand-over-fist at the expense of others. It is important to trust that 'what I have is what I need' and if I need more I can draw it to me by 'waiting on the will of my own soul'. We need to recreate a sense of wonder in a humanity that can manifest its own destiny in ways it could not have comprehended until now. Let money take care of itself.

Knowledge of how the world works will dawn on more and more people over the coming years – along with the chaos of change that these profound shifts require. Man is in for the most amazing ride of his lifetime, of any lifetime, and many people understand or suspect this from a deep well of knowing inside.

No one says it will be all smooth sailing. It requires the sacrifice of cherished dreams, in the recognition that such a dream is the stuff only of dreams in this oncoming wave of energy realignment and inner clarity.

The key to such clarity is the imagination. And once the full extent of the power of the imagination is understood and used to perceive the truth of human potential and creativity, then all will receive – without exception.

MAKING THE MOST OF THE LIFE YOU'VE GOT

In the coming months a marvellous opportunity will arise for everyone to make a commitment to a more flexible mode of living and to become aware that there is far more to life than they could possibly have imagined.

The planet is becoming more flexible in and of itself, in that there is more plasticity in the atmosphere as a result of each individual's ability to open up to the inner gaze. There will be more and more opportunity to create from the ethers exactly the kind of future we would wish for ourselves, provided the atmosphere in and around us is sufficiently clear for this plasticity to work.

That is why it is vital for each person to take responsibility for his or her own actions and reactions. Unless they do, not only will they miss out on an adventure of a lifetime, but they will also become a contaminant of the planet as a whole. As we have seen, the emotional pollution of the planet is far more dangerous and 'sticky' than any of the carbon emissions currently being pumped into the atmosphere.

The most precious commodity anyone can possess is clean air. Not in the sense of making sure every breath you take is filtered and scrubbed from the outside, but from the inside.

'Getting on' and 'getting ahead' has been the motivation for all the striving in the world today. But what if the human being has a different motive for his life from now on? What if we now know there are other more meaningful things we are meant to be pursuing in life, in order to 'make the grade'?

The most important thing at this time is to think of the *now moment*. The now moment is the most important moment of your life. Why not take a rest in time, and think of *now* as a concept for every moment of your life. *Now* is a moment of great infinity. Infinity is the world in which you live and have your being. Yet no one takes time to think of the now of infinity when there is so much else to be concerned about – making plans for an imaginary future.

'I want it and I want it now' is the prevailing attitude in life today. The demand for 'instant access' to everything you are persuaded you must experience or possess, means that *now* is only understood in a material way. It is this that has led to the precarious financial state the world is in today.

But *now* is an inner moment. It is a moment of great change, a moment of unrivalled inspiration. Now is the time for a different kind of currency dealing, so that we move and have our being in league with a sense of universal collaboration and harmony, ready to receive riches we never dreamed of.

Why not take a moment to think about this bigger picture, to think about the way we live right now, only concerned with the mundane world of men and women. Think about a world engaged in the greater meaning of mankind and the universe and all that is revolving in the wonderful movement of stars and planets – into infinity – and held in the now moment in time.

Who dares will win. Those who have the courage to sit and wait in the now moment will see themselves in the Light of mankind. A light to which no one has yet had full access because it has been the nature of humanity to yearn for more, and more, and more: more knowledge, more understanding, more goods, more services, more light, more regard.

Until now that is. It is time now to sit and ponder on what you have in the here and now, to be content with the life you've got. Right now.

What a task. What courage it takes to stop the world in the now moment; to become aware that in this pinpoint of light and time, you have all you need to be happy, to be the master of your own universal understanding of what it is to be human.

Where are you now? Where are you if you sit here now?

Put yourself in a pinpoint of light. Begin to wander around in this pinpoint of light. Allow yourself to begin to feel the influence of that pinpoint of light entering into the depth of your being, your heart, your mind, your body, your soul.

How does that feel to you, an ordinary human being, with a body and soul that is filled with light? It is time to open your eyes to who you are and what you have and where you are going, as a human being filled with light.

Cast your light for a moment. Feel that beam of light enter into the earth and feel the earth waking up to a sense of itself as a being of light, without question; a joyous feeling that becomes so broad and beautiful and deliciously sweet that your whole body responds with the pleasure of being able to do this for planet earth. Now, at this moment in time, not as a yearning or discreet wish for the future, but *now* in your own heart and mind and body.

What a turn-up! What a pleasure. I am my father's keeper and my brother's and my sister's and my children's. I can affect them for the best with this acceptance of who I am in the now moment: a Being of Light in a Light-filled world.

Why not trust it? Why not believe it? Why not make a life of it now – a real life? It's time to change. Time for a new understanding of what it is to be human in a human world filled with the Light of the World.

For more information about Annie Davison
www.guidelines.uk.com

BOOKS

O is a symbol of the world, of oneness and unity. In different cultures it also means the "eye," symbolizing knowledge and insight. We aim to publish books that are accessible, constructive and that challenge accepted opinion, both that of academia and the "moral majority."

Our books are available in all good English language bookstores worldwide. If you don't see the book on the shelves ask the bookstore to order it for you, quoting the ISBN number and title. Alternatively you can order online (all major online retail sites carry our titles) or contact the distributor in the relevant country, listed on the copyright page.

See our website **www.o-books.net** for a full list of over 500 titles, growing by 100 a year.

And tune in to myspiritradio.com for our book review radio show, hosted by June-Elleni Laine, where you can listen to the authors discussing their books.

mySpiritRadio